SCRUM Product Ownership

Balancing Value from the Inside Out

Stories, Ideas, Lessons, and Practices for Becoming a Great Product Owner

Second Edition

Robert Galen

Many of the designations used by manufacturers and sellers to distinguish their products are claimed as trademarks. Where those designations appear in this book, and the publisher was aware of the trademark claim, the designations have been printed with initial capital letters or all capitals.

The author and publisher have taken care in the preparation of this book, but make no expressed or implied warranty of any kind and assume no responsibility for errors of omission. No liability is assumed for incidental or consequential damages in connection with or arising out of the use of the information contained herein.

ISBN: 978-0-9885026-2-8

Printed in the United States

Forward to the Second Edition

I'm beginning the second edition of the book in late 2012, December to be precise. My target for publishing the second edition is Q1 2013, so I have an aggressive goal to turnaround some new insights, while keeping the best of the previous work.

The original Scrum Product Ownership (SPO) book was released in 2009, so it's been around for a bit over three years. Originally, I wrote the book because there was so little guidance surrounding the Product Owner role at the time. In fact, mine was the first book on the topic and first real effort to provide some definition for the role. That is beyond the brief illustrations from the Certified Scrum Master (CSM) class or a few articles on the Scrum Alliance site.

Fast forward to 2012, and this has fundamentally changed. There are now *two other books related to the role*[1]. The Certified Scrum Product Owner (CSPO) certification has certainly matured as has the natural web community guidance that has surfaced. All in all, you can no longer use the excuse that you don't know what's expected of the Product Owner.

But it's still not an easy role. In fact, as Agile and Scrum have increased in popularity and matured, the challenges have increased as well.

There has been an increase in the discussion surrounding 'value'. How do you select the most valuable work? And even more importantly, how do you measure value once delivered to your customers? So the notion of valuation has become more hotly explored. You even see this emerging from the lean community in books such as Eric Ries' – *The Lean Startup*[2].

---

[1] Roman Prichard's – *Agile Product Management with Scrum: Creating Products that Customers Love* and
Greg Cohen's – *Agile Excellence for Product Managers: A Guide to Creating Winning Products with Agile Development Teams*.
[2] Eric Ries – *The Lean Startup: How Today's Entrepreneurs Use Continuous Innovation to Create Radically Successful Businesses*.

Another topic area that I see ongoing in my coaching is teams and organizations struggling to 'manage' agility at scale. Activities that cause frustration and failure include: how to setup teams, how to do agile portfolio planning, how to do release planning, envisioning, coordinating testing across twenty agile teams, synchronizing work towards a deliverable, etc. How to effectively morph our entire portfolio and project level planning experience towards agile transformation seems to be an elusive goal.

The role is still incredibly broad, incredibly nuanced, and incredibly challenging for a single individual to do well. I've probably met 2-300 product owners over the last five or so years and I think perhaps 3-5 of them were doing an outstanding job across all of the aspects of the role. So we're still not setting up the Product Owner role (and the individuals) within it for success.

And finally, I've just learned a lot more. I've had three to four years of additional, in the trenches experience, and a lot more stories to tell, all of which led to my gaining momentum towards updating the book.

Modifications to the previous edition

One of the core challenges to updating the SPO book was to retain the existing mission and value. Perhaps I should start by articulating the original focus.

The original book was primarily intended to be a "Users Guide" for the Scrum Product Owner role. Given that, I took the approach of walking through the Scrum framework as a means of illustrating most of the responsibilities. I'm going to change that tack this time and focus more on operational areas for coverage.

There will be four primary sections within the book:

1. Role of the Product Owner
2. Product Backlogs
3. Scrum Sprint Dynamics and Execution
4. Product Ownership at Scale

In which I will focus the contents more along these topical boundaries. I believe it will help new readers in finding relevant guidance more easily.

I've added two new chapters, one on Scaling Agile teams and the other on Agile Project Chartering. I've also enhanced the section on agile scaling quite a bit. It was one of the areas I least focused on in the first edition and one in which I get the most questions in my classes and coaching.

I've removed all of the reference materials at the end, as I think we've moved beyond the basics. You'll see more cross-referencing though and we've even added an index to this edition.

I've added quite a few more stories and updated some. In the original book, I deferred telling my own stories to a degree. I'll share more of my personal anecdotes in this edition. You'll see quite a few from iContact, as I spent a significant amount of time there from 2009 through late 2011. It was a rich landscape of agile "done well", but with sufficient real world challenges to still be interesting. I've also tried to gather more stories from others. So the real-world story content in this edition should be significantly increased.

Virtually every chapter in the first edition has been touched in some way in my efforts; hopefully for the better. I did leave some of the initial dates within the text, but don't feel they overly date the material. I honestly feel this edition brings the book up to 2013 in "State of the Art" Scrum Product Ownership.

I hope you find value within the covers.

Bob.

Contents

Acknowledgements

First of all, I want to thank all of the Scrum teams I've worked with in my consulting practice and, most recently, ChannelAdvisor; particularly the Product Owners. I've learned so many wonderful things about agility and how teams adapt to their contexts. It's also been incredibly enjoyable to be welcomed into these teams and be part of the energy that encompasses agile methods adoption. I'm extremely blessed to be part of each and every instance.

Secondly, I need to thank Henrik Kniberg. His _Scrum and XP from the Trenches_ book has been a true inspiration for this one. I remember when Henrik first _threw_ his book out on various discussion groups and made it freely available. I immediately downloaded a copy and it became a favorite agile reference of mine both personally and for recommending to my clients.

I found it highly practical and chock full of real-world advice; something that is often missing in many of the agile references and the community at-large. If I can provide even a small part of the value that Henrik achieved in his guide, I will be more than pleased with my efforts in giving something back to the agile community.

I also want to thank my early reviewers. To be honest with you, I'm quite nervous about releasing this into the broad agile community. I needed to get some early feedback to gain confidence. These early reviewers were gracious enough to provide time and feedback and I'm extremely grateful for every bit of it.

A heartfelt thank you to: Carlos Alvarez, John Baker, **Tony Brill, **Shaun Bradshaw, **Michael Faisst, **Mike Hall, Margaret Menzies, **Rich Mironov, Roman Pichler and Bas Vodde;

** - contributed 'stories' to the text, so an extra _thank you_ to them.

Most importantly, I want to thank my family for putting up with yet another, albeit shorter, book project. Bug—as always, all my love and you're simply the best! To Da Boys, and Da Kids all my love too…

And for the 2'nd Edition

I want to take time to thank my primary "inspiration" for the past 3+ years. By that I mean, where do the new experiences and approaches come from? In my case, they come from my coaching, whether it's teams that I'm directly a part of or external coaching clients. My inspiration comes from the real world, including frustrations, challenges, patterns, and anti-patterns.

My inspiration directly came from:

- My 2 ½ years at iContact
- Numerous coaching clients
- Discussions during my Meta-casts with Josh Anderson
- Interactions at conferences and training workshops
- Some work history with Teradata and ChannelAdvisor
- Our local Raleigh/Durham agile community
- And finally a short, but rich, stint at Deutsche Bank

I want to thank everyone that I've worked with on agile adoption. I honor your efforts, intentions, and everything I've learned from you. You've helped me to continually improve my agile coaching and servant leadership.

For 2 ½ years I was fortunate and lucky enough to help build and coach just such a set of teams at iContact. In many ways, I wouldn't be the coach I am today without the opportunity to partner with this group. It was a distinct privilege to work with such fine agilists. From where I sit, we were very much...hyper-performing!

In particular at iContact I want to thank Ralph Kasuba for giving me the chance to lead such a wonderful team. Ralph is one of my role models for servant leadership done well and I greatly appreciated his trust and empowerment.

So, at the risk of leaving someone off the list, I want to thank these iContact folks for helping continuously reframe my agile coaching. Thanks to, Maureen Green, Tim Kykendall, Anne Moore, Jackie Owino, Andrew Parker, Bill Bates, David Rasch, Mark Riedeman, Brian Sobus, and Mary Thorn.

Also thanks to our U/X team and our Product Team led by Michelle Engle. Our wonderful Product Owners included: Michelle, Peter Ghali, Rob Call, Alan Cox, Matt Davis, Eddie Howard, Jeff Ravetto, and Jeff Wright.

I want to thank my early reviewers: Craig McCrary, Michael Faisst, Chris DeNardis, Anand Srinivasan, and Cory Bryan; particularly Craig who went above and beyond in providing detailed feedback despite fighting a back injury.

I also want to again thank my family. My children have always been incredibly supportive of what I do. And my wife Diane has been a constant and tireless supporter. Diane, your patience and support now and always mean the world to me. Thank you all for supporting what I love to do.

For those who know me, you know that Diane and I are fairly rabid pet lovers. During the time I was collecting my thoughts for the second edition, we lost our beloved dog Foster. We love ALL of our animals dearly. But Foster was special to us. He was more human than dog and we treasured the time we had with him.

I'm quite positive he had a strong influence (and still does) on my agile coaching and writing. We miss you Fost-man!

And last but not least, I want to thank you for picking up this book, your interest in my thoughts, and for taking time out of your busy day. I hope you find something of value within…to help you in your own journey.

Stay agile my friends…

Chapter 1

Introduction

There are many Scrum Product Owners and/or agile customers who feel their job solely revolves around creating a Product Backlog or list of prioritized features for their product development efforts. While all of the agile methodologies are essentially driven by such a list, there is an incredible amount of nuance and breadth beyond this to getting the role 'right'.

I've spent the past few years working with many companies, coaching their agile teams towards more effective product development, and quite often they had adopted this attitude. Sure, the Product Owners engaged with their teams, but it wasn't always heartfelt or fully focused. Some of their common behaviors included:

- Providing not much more than a high level, ordered backlog and limited availability to the team for questions or clarification.
- User stories were developed, but were inconsistent and refined too late; often in sprint planning.
- Intermittent development of sprint goals and rarely were they truly unique or compelling.
- Backlog grooming (maintenance) was inconsistently practiced, if practiced at all.
- The backlogs themselves were inconsistent across teams, which made organizational strategic planning and overall progress measurement quite difficult.
- Forward-looking release planning was nearly avoided—preferring *Sprint-at-a-Time* thinking.
- Little time was spent 'connecting' external stakeholders to the performance, efforts, and dynamics of their teams.

It wasn't their entire fault either. They were often Product Managers within the organization who were overloaded with numerous tasks that fell outside of their Scrum team responsibilities. They often seemed conflicted with their time, focus and motivation.

As we executed Scrum across many teams and organizations, I noticed emergent patterns. Some of the teams seemed to struggle all of the time, barely completing their sprints, and often missing their overall sprint goals. Mark my words carefully—they failed! Geez...that's not supposed to happen within agile teams!

Conversely, some teams performed much better than others and consistently over-delivered on their promises. They often created functionality that was simple and struck to the heart of their customers' needs. Their code was straightforward and of high quality and seemed to have very few bugs. I'd even say a few of these teams ventured into the hyper-productive arena that Jeff Sutherland and others so often *illustrate* [3] as the agile *nirvana state*.

Upon closer observation a set of patterns, approaches, and techniques emerged that I believe represent the approaches, behaviors and attitudes of **Great Product Owners**. It is these observations that I want to share with you in this book. Clearly, not all of them will apply to you in your contexts. However, it is my hope that they will encourage you to try new approaches and/or find a renewed determination and focus in your role as a Product Manager, Product Owner, and Customer Advocate.

The Books' Context

The title of the book emphasizes a focus of "From the Inside Out". What do I mean by that? I mean that nearly every conversation within centers on your interactions with your Agile or Scrum team first. I'm certainly not downplaying the importance of being customer or externally facing as a Product Owner. In fact, that *is* your "Prime Directive". However, I've seen so many Scrum Product Owners that that's all they do.

They collaborate with customers and stakeholders; they're on the road three weeks out of four, and then, they're doing product demos the remainder of the time. All along, their teams are drowning without them!

While I honor how difficult this role is, I want to emphasize the characteristics of a great Product Owner as they engage their teams "in the moment" of sprinting. That before you look externally, you've established a partnership with your team and are spending sufficient time with them; or at

---

[3] Sutherland has spoken and written at length about his experiences while at PatientKeeper. He alludes to his team's achieving 200-300% performance improvements over their Waterfall counterparts.

the very least, are providing the backlog, goals, and real-time feedback they need.

I'm also assuming that you have some basic knowledge and experience in Scrum. That you've operated as, or worked closely with, a Product Owner in creating a product backlog or two and witnessed it's execution through a Scrum team. That you've seen the potential within Scrum teams and see them as a means towards creating great products by collaboration and a focus on quality execution.

I'm also making the assumption, and a very generous one, that you've already defined your business and marketing goals for your Scrum project(s) so, all of that up-front work has been completed. From a marketing perspective, here are some of the things that would/should have already occurred, particularly if you're focused on *product* development efforts—

- Defined the target market
- Identify intended customer(s) and sales channel(s)
- Clearly articulate the top few benefits
- Establish a simple version of a pricing/revenue model

This is sort of the minimal set of marketing tasks that need to be completed before tasking a Scrum team with product development work. I'm assuming that someone in the organization, perhaps the Director of Product Management or Chief Product Owner, has established a sound business foundation for beginning your project.

Beyond product development, you may be working as part of an internal development function within an IT organization. While much of your focus is the same as the product focused team, you often have a somewhat captured market and revenue stream driven from your internal customers.

From the Inside Out

Again, with my "in the moment" perspective, we're not going to spend much time discussing project preparatory activities. Instead, my assumption is that you have a well understood and characterized project that has just begun implementation to leverage Scrum and Agile dynamics. So, you're essentially *diving in*.

Diving in with your initial focus being—the team. Looking to see how your role merges with theirs. Learning how to feed their backlog and provide high quality customer feedback. Discovering their delivery capabilities and effectively managing stakeholder expectations. Providing a compelling vision for what your customers need and why they need to build it as specified. Sharing challenges in such a way that it motivates the team with enthusiasm and energy.

Yes, you need to be customer facing and yes, you need to intimately understand their needs. But, in order to deliver towards those needs, your team is your first priority. Only they can help you deliver great products—from the inside out.

Recommended Reading Flow

If you're new to the role of Product Owner, then I think a sequential reading of the book will probably add the most value for you.

If you're an experienced Product Owner, then I think Section 1 is optional for you. I would advise taking a peek though.

I've added an index to the 2'nd Edition of the book, so that might be a way of discovering point topics and uncovering advice for your specific questions or challenges.

I spent quite a lot of time adding additional information and references in the footnotes. I recommend not skipping over them in your haste, as I think there's great value there.

Core Scrum Practices

At the time of writing this second edition, there's been a crescendo of debate in the Scrum community, particularly among the CST's (Certified Scrum Trainers), around what are core Scrum practices versus what are not.

For example, there are very few CST's who 'like' the notion of a Sprint #0. There are two parts to their disdain. I think number one is using Scrum terminology, which inherently implies that something is a "part of" Scrum. In listening to them, I realized that we shouldn't mix terminology. So, we could call a Sprint #0 a George #0, and everyone would be fine with that distinction.

The second part of the issue is with the tactic itself. Many of them view the Sprint #0 as a means of breaking the essence of a central Scrum tenant. In this case, completing a sprint without any discernible software delivered. So, from a Lean perspective, it can be very 'wasteful'.

I'm not trying to argue the merits of Sprint #0's here, just explain the aspects of a contention point as an example.

I liken these Scrum trainers and leaders into two camps. There are the purists, who will spend hours and days discussing the right length of the time-box for a Sprint Planning meeting. Or whether it is better to "commit to" a sprint or "forecast a" sprint as a team. I find them passionate, but incredibly dogmatic in their interpretation of Scrum. I also find that it's too purist and truly un-helpful for many teams struggling in gaining traction in "real world" contexts. But they're not necessarily bad people, just purists.

Then there are the pragmatists, who are much more flexible in the application and adjustment of agile practices. While the end result might night be "perfect Agile" or "perfect Scrum", the results are usually _far better_ than the organization and teams had achieved with previous approaches.

For the purposes of this book, I will go on record as being a "pragmatist" and as such, I run the risk of aggravating the purists. I'm relatively ok with that.

How do you get to the "Core"?

It turns out that there are relatively easy ways to understand what Core Scrum is. Unfortunately, the "bad news" is that there are two distinct definitions:

1. If you come from the Scrum Alliance side of things, then the Agile Atlas is the core reference for core Scrum.
2. If you come from the Scrum.org side of things, then the Scrum Guide is the central reference for core Scrum.

Ron Jeffries leads the group collaborating around the Agile Atlas and this is a sponsored effort by the Scrum Alliance.

Ken Schwaber and Jeff Sutherland are the authors behind the Scrum Guide. Jeff is also a CST, so there is some overlap between them.

My Intentions

Here are my intentions for representing Scrum practices in the book.
First, I want to share things that I've seen work. Whether they fall into the
core or not, I'll share stories, lessons, and techniques that I've seen work
quite well in Scrum and other agile instances. Not just in one instance, but
many times. It's up to you to decide whether the concepts will work in your
contexts. You need to think. You also need to differentiate between core
Scrum and what are often referred to as GASPS – Generally Accepted
Scrum Practices.

There are some clear GASP's that I'll discuss in the book, they include:

1. User Stories
2. Hardening and Stabilization focused sprints
3. Leveraging a Sprint #0 or an Iteration #0
4. Release Planning and Blitz Planning
5. Various estimation techniques
6. Lean techniques for Minimal Marketable goals
7. Agile chartering
8. Product Owners being a member of the Scrum team and attending
   all ceremonies
9. Performing architecture and design in a sprint-ahead fashion
10. Leveraging a Scrum of Scrums for scaling

And I'm sure there are more. My intent is NOT to be controversial nor buck
the Scrum Core. It's simply to bring my experiences to bear and to let you
be the judge on what's useful.

You see, I firmly believe that context matters!

And finally, A Call to Arms

Finally, there are a number of impediments that stand in the way of Product Owners becoming great; many of them are outside their control. I fully acknowledge this as well as the fact that the role is so broadly challenging.

My perspective in all of this is not to judge, but simply one of trying to *Raise the Bar* for the Product Owner role; independent of your challenges or impediments. Your performance is crucial to a team's success and I feel that Product Owners, regardless of how conflicted, have a responsibility to their teams to step onto the path to becoming great.

This guide is intended to outline these characteristics of greatness and set the expectation that every Product Owner needs to raise the breadth and depth of their performance.

If a single Product Owner cannot perform all of the functions that I'm outlining within, then it is their responsibility to put together a team that can meet these demands. To do anything less would risk reducing their and their team's agile performance to mere mediocrity.

So, become great for yourself, your teams, your organization and so that you DELIVER on the incredible promise of agility!

Remembering the quote:

"With Great Power Comes Great Responsibility"

Happy Product Ownership!

Bob Galen
Cary, NC—Spring 2013

Section 1

The Role of the Product Owner

There are four chapters in this section focused towards establishing the basic role definition of the Product Owner.

Chapter 2 – 'Role' of the Product Owner
Here we explore the fundamental role description of the Product Owner and the notion of going it alone versus taking a village approach to the role.

Chapter 3 – Basics of the Role
The chapter focuses more on skill set requirements; the depth, breadth, and subtlety of the role, and again, how challenging it is for any single individual to fill.

Chapter 4 – The Product Owner as Leader
Whether you like it or not, the Product Owner role is a leader role. They play a key role in influencing the performance of the team and in directing their product results.

Chapter 5 – Understanding How Your Role Influences Quality
One of the basic misunderstandings about agile is that it's a "speed play". Instead, the reality is that it's a "quality play" that can potentially go "fast". The Product Owner is central to agile teams holding to their quality goals.

Chapter 2

The 'Role' of the Product Owner

One of my primary drivers for writing this book was to illustrate the breadth of the Product Owner role to ensure that _someone_ fills in all of the various aspects. I think that's the most crucial point.

I want to share the current definition of the Product Owner role by Ken Schwaber and Jeff Sutherland in their **Scrum Guide**[4]:

> The Product Owner is responsible for maximizing the value of the product and the work of the Development Team. How this is done may vary widely across organizations, Scrum Teams, and individuals.
>
> The Product Owner is the sole person responsible for managing the Product Backlog. Product Backlog management includes:
>
> - Clearly expressing Product Backlog items;
> - Ordering the items in the Product Backlog to best achieve goals and missions;
> - Ensuring the value of the work the Development Team performs;
> - Ensuring that the Product Backlog is visible, transparent, and clear to all, and shows what the Scrum Team will work on next; and,
> - Ensuring the Development Team understands items in the Product Backlog to the level needed.
>
> The Product Owner may do the above work, or have the Development Team do it. However, the Product Owner remains accountable.

---

[4] Scrum Guide, October 2011 version, except from page 5
http://www.scrum.org/Scrum-Guides

The Product Owner is one person, not a committee. The Product Owner may represent the desires of a committee in the Product Backlog, but those wanting to change a backlog item's priority must convince the Product Owner.

For the Product Owner to succeed, the entire organization must respect his or her decisions. The Product Owner's decisions are visible in the content and ordering of the Product Backlog. No one is allowed to tell the Development Team to work from a different set of requirements, and the Development Team isn't allowed to act on what anyone else says.

Again from the **Scrum Guide**[5], Schwaber and Sutherland share on the collaborative responsibilities that the Scrum Master has with the Product Owner.

Scrum Master Service to the Product Owner
The Scrum Master serves the Product Owner in several ways, including:

- Finding techniques for effective Product Backlog management;
- Clearly communicating vision, goals, and Product Backlog items to the Development Team;
- Teaching the Scrum Team to create clear and concise Product Backlog items;
- Understanding long-term product planning in an empirical environment;
- Understanding and practicing agility; and,
- Facilitating Scrum events as requested or needed.

[5] Scrum Guide, October 2011 version, except from page 7
http://www.scrum.org/Scrum-Guides

There Can Be Only One!

As I sit updating this chapter in the fall of *2012*[6], there have been some heated debates on the discussion groups and blogs regarding whether a single or group Product Owner best meets the team's needs. A response from Ken Schwaber stated that there is "Only ONE Product Owner". A part of me wonders if there's more to the story than that pronouncement. Surely, there are contexts where a single individual may not have the time or capability to perform all aspects of the role, particularly the broad role I allude to in the next chapter. What do you do in those cases? Not do it? Or do you force a person to do something they are not capable of doing? I certainly hope not.

I think the distinction here is, and perhaps Ken is saying this as well, is that there is a *single responsible person*, a Product Owner for each Scrum team. Zero or more than one person is not an option here, as this one person needs to be ultimately responsible for decision-making from a business perspective.

Now that doesn't mean there can't be other individuals, who are engaged with, and helping the Product Owner with aspects of the role where the Product Owner is weak or lacks the time to accomplish them. And I'm not referring to a loosely coupled committee here which fosters consensus only decision-making. For example, as a Scrum Master I foster the idea that the team is responsible for the quality of the backlog and not solely the Product Owner.

If important quality steps, for example refactoring critical components or repairing important bugs aren't on backlog, then it's the team's responsibility to craft good stories that represent that work. They, in some fashion, become the "Product Owner" for these specific, more technical stories. They also craft the acceptance criteria and balance the effort for these stories against the more business focused stories. Thus partnering with the Product Owner to create a more balanced and healthy backlog. But that doesn't mean they 'own' the overall responsibility.

As a Scrum Master, I often jump in and help with the backlog grooming activity. In fact, I often spend the majority of my time doing work that I think classically falls under the purview of the Product Owner. Why;

---

[6] And it's still a subject for debate in late 2012

because it's necessary for the team to get the job done. It's also part of the natural partnership between Scrum Master and Product Owner.

The two key questions regarding the Product Ownership coverage dynamics are:

1. Are central activities being effectively covered?
2. Is there a single decision-making voice?

If you have those answers, then to my way of thinking, much of the discussion and debate surrounding singular versus group Product Ownership melts away.

Always Have To Be a Product Manager?

There is a strong trend in many organizations moving to Scrum where market-focused Product Managers are designated as Product Owners. That becomes the default assignment; even in cases where a single Product Owner can have multiple teams collaborating on shared or integrated code for a single product.

This can really overload the Product Manager/Owner. There are a couple of team roles that I've seen become useful in supplementing the Product Owner role. First is the software testing or QA team members. They can provide tremendous assistance refining user stories and providing acceptance tests; focusing the team on these efforts. In fact, this is a healthy and common shift for most testers, moving their focus *up-stream* to provide clarity and improve quality at the requirements level.

If you have Business Analysts within your organization, they too can become partners in this requirements definition and refinement process. The Product Owner can't become too complacent and disengaged, but at the same time, having team members who are really skilled with requirement-centric work makes good sense.

I'd also like to make the argument that nearly anyone with connections to the true customer (or the customer themselves) can make a great Product Owner. It really depends on your context and the needs of the team, with the key point being it doesn't always have to be the Product Manager. Certainly they will be part of the solution, but perhaps due to their business-facing focus, they can play more of a backseat role to someone else with a different skill-set.

Conflicts with Product Management as a Profession

I've been in quite a few situations where I became frustrated with my Product Owners not taking adequate time with their teams. Until just recently, I thought it was mostly a choice they were making. Sure, they had a few outwardly focused tasks and needed to communicate with many types of internal and external customers, but certainly they had more time for their teams! I mean really, how much more was there for them to do?

Then I began studying the role of the Product Manager as it relates to the Product Owner. There's a wonderful group called *Pragmatic Marketing*[7] that offers training, consulting and guidance for the profession of Product Marketing, as well as, other aspects of more technical marketing. They've devised a model entitled the Pragmatic Marketing Framework that illustrates all of the aspects and activities of Marketing Product Management.

What's interesting is that the role of Product Owner only covers about 8-10 of the total 37 responsible areas of operation for the Product Management role. Many of these additional responsibility areas focus on company leadership driven areas, such as strategic product alignment. Imagine you're a Product Manager/Owner and you inform the CEO that you can't do the strategic market analysis he needs for the board because your agile teams need you to work on the backlog. Which one do you think should get your attention?

No wonder we have _tension_ in the agile community where we have Product Owners who are struggling to balance their roles against organizational Product Management expectations.

I now have a newfound respect for the position of the Product Manager and Owner and, in most cases, recommend that they create a healthy, *collaborative group* [8]to fill in all aspects of these roles as required. Because

---

[7] www.pragmaticmarketing.com is an extremely well respected firm in this space. They've partnered with Luke Hohmann's firm Enthiosys (www.enthiosys.com) to increase their focus on Agile Product Ownership vs. Product Marketing and Management.

[8] Chapter 19 is focused on the Organizational Dynamics of scaling the Product organization in agile contexts. Part of the discussion in this chapter is setting up structures of outwardly facing Product Managers and inwardly facing Product Owners—creating a Product hierarchy that effectively supports ALL aspects of the role.

no good comes from a great Product Owner who becomes a terminated or burned-out Product Owner!

Additional Product Marketing Nuance

Rich Mironov, one of my early reviewers, worked for Enthiosys, an agile marketing firm founded by Luke Hohmann. He has also actively partnered with Pragmatic Marketing to extend their models and training to include more agile marketing concepts.

Rich, rightfully, took exception to my "in-the-moment" start-up assumption for the Product Owner role. He reminded me that getting the product well defined in the beginning is central to a successful project or product development; he wanted to ensure that I made this point early on. I absolutely agree with him!

If my focus for this book was broader, I'd gladly speak on such issues and challenges. In order to include a bit more focus on his sage advice, I thought I'd include a few snippets below. Please read them carefully. Rich is 100% right in his council and you will want to carefully consider his points.

Rich's Story – Don't Forget Product Marketing

Role Clarity

Yes, a Product Owner IS part Product Manager. If you don't have a full-time Product Manager assigned and you ship products to customers for revenue, you will need someone to cover the entire product management role. That's typically a long to-do list which includes segmentation, pricing, packaging, messaging, benefits/features, coordinating with Marketing / Sales / Training / Support, etc. Immediately ask for needed resources. Either you can do this or, perhaps, a junior Product Manager who will work with or for the Product Owner.

You may be assuming that a Product Manager is already assigned and has helped set up the group. In which case, you'll need to decide which PM-like things the Product Owner will do, and which things the Product Manager will do. In my experience, the Product Manager performs all of the Product Owner's role responsibilities along with several others. That's quite different from the Product Owner learning to be a part-time PM on the job.

By skipping this bit of organization, or assuming the Product Owner can simply "do it all", gets the project off on completely the wrong foot.

Importance of Strategy

You're begging the question of where business value comes from, and who frames the problem. In my honest opinion, most Product Owners have no training or experience with pricing, packaging or actual revenue value (hard dollars); they use vague hand-waving to decide what they think is valuable. Again, a technically astute and trained Product Manager (having spent time talking to customers every week), will have a well-tuned idea of what customers will pay for and what would be an unpaid requirement for the product.

It's also important to have a company-wide strategy and a division-level product strategy. Product Owners need to understand how their products fit into the overall story, as well as, drive value for the overall company. This usually has only a partial alignment with product-level options. Product Owners, who prioritize only for their individual products, can miss half of the overall value and, therefore, miss all of the opportunities to leverage the rest of their company.

To sum up: It is not practical (or smart or effective) to have the Scrum Development Team work on a revenue product and then try to discover market facts while also building software. Instead, your company-wide and division-wide strategies are critical to understanding business value(s). A Product Owner who doesn't start here will often mislead the team and over-value product-specific features versus company needs, fit, architecture, standards, EOL planning, etc.

Nor is it practical to drive business value and feature selection decisions solely from reactions from a small set of customers and/or stakeholders at periodic Sprint Reviews. It's simply not a wide enough data set to make good market decisions.

—Rich Mironov

Rich nicely makes the point that the Product Owner role is a broad one and that Product Marketing plays a key role in quantifying and qualifying your projects before injecting them into a Scrum team. I think both points play well throughout the book.

A Clearly Defined Role

Many organizations are also making a huge mistake when it comes to staffing the Product Owner role. In some cases, they overload Product Owners with many teams and force them into part-time roles. In others, they ask the team to figure it out on their own, or assign a Product Owner that doesn't have the requisite skills to be successful. These organizations need to realize that skilled Product Owners are a full-time and critical component of their agile adoption strategies' success. That lessening their investment or trivializing the role is a quick path to failure.

The Product Owner role also needs better definition. It's superficially defined in the Scrum Guide and general literature; leaving you pretty much on your own to figure out the subtleties of the role. This short guide is intended to define what, I think, are the critical requirements (skills, capabilities, strengths, and patterns) of a great Product Owner.

It is intended to provide some "depth" to the role and drive the thinking process when Product Owners are being hired into, or staffed within, agile teams. The point is: it's the most difficult job within the Scrum team and needs to be taken seriously. Product Owners need to be highly skilled individuals who understand the nuance of the role. Individuals who are enabled by the organization to take the time necessary to fully engage their teams in value-based delivery.

In order for Scrum and its associated teams to perform up to their true promise, we need to find and develop great Product Owners for these teams. Essentially the rest of the book explores the many dimensions and skills within the role.

Trusted and Empowered?

One of the core tenants of Lean and the Agile Methods is the notion of self-directed teams. This implies, amongst other things, that you have hired good people with the skills <u>and</u> experience you need to get the job done.

Therefore, as a member of the organization and leadership team, you must trust the team to do their jobs and not micro-manage them. In fact, instead of the team serving you, leadership should be consistently looking to adopt a Servant Leadership mindset and drive performance by serving the team.

Of course, as the Product Owner you <u>do</u> provide direction and guidance; however, it is more so at the vision and goal-setting levels. Once you provide clear direction, simply stay out of their way and support their journey towards achieving those goals.

That is at an agile team level. However beyond the team, it is extremely important for the organization to trust their Product Owner's abilities and skills, while enabling them to make decisions and drive their products' successful delivery. The following story or concern shared by one of my early reviewers brings this point nicely home.

Shaun's Story – Product Owner Decision-Making

As I read this section, I was reminded of a recent problem I've seen with Product Owners that I hope you will address. One of the most common complaints I've been hearing lately from scrum teams, is problems with Product Owners not being able to make decisions quickly enough. It seems they feel as if they have to check with others before making even the most trivial of decisions.

This is usually attributed to executive management not providing them with the ultimate authority to do so; they feel like they need to get approval before they can make any decision. In fact, I've recommended that one of my clients not pursue their agile adoption at that time because of this predicament. It obviously causes issues with prioritization and timely completion of work when questions cannot be answered immediately.

This is probably a common issue at other organizations and I hope you can address what a Product Owner should/might do in situations where they don't feel they have been given enough authority to fully implement the role. Some possible approaches as I see them include—

1) Ask forgiveness, not permission – make the decision then let executives find out later (you need a lot of courage for this one);
2) Have Scrum Master intervene with executives to ensure authority is given (especially useful if Scrum Master is an outside consultant);
3) Educate and/or train executives to learn why authority for Product Owners is so important.

—Shaun Bradshaw

Shaun hits the mark here on a very common problem in many early adoption agile teams. The organization is accustomed to command-and-control style management tactics which can totally undermine the effectiveness and impact of agility. Nowhere is this more destructive than in the role of the Product Owner.

His ideas for approaching the problem are relatively sound too. I personally lean towards 2 or 3 as the better approaches. I'd also ask myself if there is something being hidden from the Product Owner causing this behavior. For example: is the team not transparent enough to senior leadership? Or, are there some critical business drivers or priorities that are causing the behavior? Or, is it simply a lack of confidence in the Product Owner?

Getting to "root cause" behind your stakeholders' behavior can often be helpful in sorting through next step corrective actions.

Wrapping Up

❖ With all respect, I think Ken Schwaber is wrong or too purist in his thinking about having "Only 1" Product Owner for all contexts. While having a single Product Owner who has the time and skill to perform all aspects of the position is ideal, real-world dynamics rarely allow for that. What's much more import is whether all aspects of the role have adequate coverage by 'someone' with appropriate skill and time.

❖ In lieu of a full-time PO, ensuring that there is a single, decision maker and distributed coverage of <u>all aspects</u> of the role throughout the broader team can be a very effective alternative. Point is: don't get stuck in purist thinking. Use common sense and collaboration to get the job done.

❖ And when you're scaling the Product Owner organization, think of it in broad terms when establishing skills and responsibilities.

Chapter 3

Basics of the Role

First, I want to establish that the great Product Owner is a member of the team. Not all of the agile pundits would agree with this view, as the role is somewhat specialized in Scrum. However, setting the stage that your primary customer is your team and that you need to respond to them first, will set the stage for the *thinking model* of a great Product Owner.

Product Owners are not on the sidelines of the team; feeding them requirements and judging their output. Nor, are they presenting team results to stakeholders in a project management or reporting capacity. Instead, they are a distinct member of the team in which overall success, or failure, is a joint endeavor. The point is they've got some *skin in the game*!

This partnership also creates a firmer relationship between the Product Owner and team that enhances their collaboration and results. The team connects to the Product Owner and endeavors to deliver business value not only for the business, but because they believe in, and fully support their *customer(s) and teammate(s)*.

Ken Schwaber, one of the co-creators of Scrum, defines the role of the Product Owner as the *"Single Wring-able Neck[9]"*. What he's implying is that the Product Owner is a critical role to gain Scrum success arguably, the most important role. Secondly, that the role is part of the team; if the team 'fails', so should the Product Owner. Conversely, if the team 'succeeds', so should the Product Owner. The two should become inextricably linked.

Beyond the importance of the role, it's also a leadership role. Scrum is setup, as are all of the Agile Methodologies, so that the *customer drives* the team's focus. In this case, the Product Owner is synonymous with the

---

[9] There's been an incredible amount of debate in the Scrum community about the use of this phrase. I seriously considered deleting it from the 2'nd Edition of the book. However, I still think it powerfully makes the point of the accountability and responsibility of the Product Owner role within Scrum teams. Please look beyond any offense, and see it as a metaphor.

customer and this brings with it tremendous leadership and guidance *responsibility*[10]!

The third point I feel Schwaber is making is that the team depends on the Product Owner to give them the "*right things to do*". They expect that you're working diligently with customers and stakeholders to quantify and qualify the feature set that will bring the greatest value to the business and the team's efforts.

I've worked with some Product Owners who felt that they completely understood their markets and drove their teams down a path towards project and product delivery. They did little in advanced qualification of the work or showing their customers early sprint reviews to gain feedback. From their perspective, why ask when you *know* what the customers need.

However, when the projects were finally vetted with real clients, they received the traditional feedback that frightens most Waterfall projects: "This isn't what we asked for." Or, "This is useless, we don't work this way".

One of the more important responsibilities of a great Product Owner is to ensure that they've done everything possible to qualify the work their teams are delivering. Ensuring that it meets customer and business needs, not by perception or assumption, but by listening to customers, engaging in frequent demonstrations, and embracing and reacting to feedback!

A Breadth of Experience

Another basic view is directed towards the *breadth of the role*[11]. We'll get into details later, but I want to explore this early on. The Product Owner in my mind is:

- **Part Product Manager:** Deeply and broadly understanding the business needs for their particular product(s). Continuously talking to customers and gathering information about their wants and needs. Communicating outward regarding team, product, and project

---

[10] So much so that I devote an entire chapter to it – Chapter 4.

[11] In a recent Meta-cast, Josh and I explored the notion of a Quadrant-based view to the role of the Product Owner. His premise was – why do we need Product Owners. You can listen to the conversation here: http://www.meta-cast.com/2012/12/episode-31-who-needs-product-owners.html

"state" to customers and stakeholders. Creating a shared vision for where the market is going and how to leverage that opportunity. Translating that vision into the features and dynamics for a product and mapping it into "chunks or themes" for each release.

- **Part Project Manager:** This is more from a forward thinking product roadmap perspective. They help guide work iteration tempo as it relates to the forecast versus team velocity and release schedule. Often accomplished by building a plan towards market release timing that includes: product quality goals and testing, documentation, support training, sales training, marketing preparation, operations and deployment needs, etc. Creating and negotiating the steps leading to a successful release point.

- **Part Leader:** Serving as a focal point within the team. Motivating team members by providing compelling goals and objectives. Being able to make hard choices on priority and business value. Guiding, motivating, and listening to their teams in finding creative ways to *deliver more value with less scope and effort*. Defending their team and removing relevant impediments. Coming to understand what their team's strengths are and leveraging them to advantage in project workflow.

- **Part Business Analyst:** This is the requirement writing aspect of the role, defining artifacts (use cases, user stories, or traditional requirement artifacts) for the team to carry out. Often defining acceptance tests and measurements for 'done-ness'. A good part of this is to foster collaboration between architects, developers, testers, and themselves.

Since the skill requirements are so broad and intimidating, this might be why the role is so difficult to staff with a single individual and why the business minimizes it so often. I also think this is why a cobbled-together Product Owner approach is instantiated in many teams, as no single individual can provide the requisite breadth in skill.

Earlier, I may have implied that the cobbled-together Product Owner, i.e., multiple team members who assume aspects of the role, might be a bad idea. I actually think it can be a healthy alternative as long as ALL aspects of the role are covered and a single person assumes the "Primary" Product

Ownership role—so, there is only one accountable Product Owner without any contention or external confusion.

Two External References

It might be useful to share two external perspectives on the overview of the Product Owner role. First is *a list* [12] by Laszlo Szalvy that speaks to the top seven responsibilities of the role:

Laszlo Szalvy: Top 7 Scrum Product Owner Responsibilities

1. Leads the development effort by conveying his or her vision to the team and outlining work in the Scrum backlog.
2. Prioritizes work based on Business Value.
3. Negotiates work with the team.
4. Must remain available to the team to answer questions and deliver direction.
5. Must resist the temptation to micromanage.
6. Must resist "raiding the team's spirit."
7. Must not be afraid to make tough decisions.

I particularly like #6. I've seen many Product Owners that don't honor their teams and make decisions that "raid their spirit". For example, ignoring team recommendations for defect repairs or refactoring needs; instead, pushing a feature-only release pattern in the backlog. This sort of narrow focus can quickly demoralize a team and clearly doesn't support self-organization.

Roman Pichler: Key Points to Product Owner Effectiveness

Another *reference* [13] is by a competing author. Roman Pichler published a Scrum Product Owner book about a year after the first edition of this book was published. In an article on the Scrum Alliance website, Roman expanded on these core role responsibilities:

---

[12] Here's a link – http://top7business.com/?id=11111
[13] Here's a link – http://www.scrumalliance.org/articles/44-being-an-effective-product-owner

First, closely collaborate with the team on an ongoing basis and to guide and direct the team:

- By actively managing the product backlog,
- Answering questions when they arise,
- Providing feedback, and
- Signing off on work results.

In simple terms, the product owner sits in the driver's seat, deciding what should be done and when the software should be shipped.

I have found three things particularly helpful for product owners:

1. A thorough understanding of the customer needs,
2. Active stakeholder management, and
3. A basic knowledge of how software is developed and deployed.

Both Laszlo and Roman do a nice job of capturing their perspectives, and valid ones, on the central themes for effective product ownership.

One important area that they missed, although Roman mentioned "active stakeholder management", was in the external communications and expectations management role that the Product Owner needs to play for their team. In its purest sense, I view the role as "*360° Marketing*" of your teams focus, efforts, challenges, and results in a fully transparent way.

Sure the Scrum Master has external communications as one of their core responsibilities as well. But two can be more effective than one.

Essence of the Role

Finally, the basic focus of the Product Owner within the team is product backlog generation and coordination. This is realized by first creating a backlog and then, during the course of project events, changing the priority and flow to reflect the team and customer's needs for the product or project. An important part of this is defining sprint-level and release-level goals that drive the team forward; presenting a compelling, higher level vision for the implementation timing and basic customer needs for the project.

This simple view is the _essence_ of the role of the Product Owner, which may lead to creating an overly simplistic view to the work. I actually find that many Product Owners fall into the trap that managing the backlog is _all_ they have to do, which undermines the complexity and nuance of the role.

Another one of my early reviewers shared with me the following story that highlights his personal observations and challenges related to the variability in the role of Product Owner. I thought it might be good to share it now in this section to illustrate another person's view to critical success factors regarding the Product Owner roles focus:

A Challenge and Ability to "Shift Gears" Story

I think that the challenges of shifting gears between road maps and backlogs and internal stakeholders versus external stakeholders, are among the toughest ones - at least for me. Many Product Managers I have seen come from a pure marketing background and tend to have less affinity with engineering, sometimes resulting in challenged and limited communication. One of the trials I see is that Product Managers in the role of Product Owners are having to bridge between Product Backlog and Sprint Planning versus Product Marketing and Strategic Planning.

One is aimed at optimal performance while the other is aimed at predictability of annual deliveries. Marketing and executive teams want to know what will be released 12, or even 24, months from now and will actively plan market activities and revenue projections around those deliveries. Whereas the input from Scrum planning only provides us predictability for the near future, a successful Product Owner needs to manage expectations both ways and be able to shift between these two very different views. Shifting their focus without burdening one team too heavily with expectations of the other yet, always maintaining their transparency.

This becomes especially challenging when estimating Product Backlog items further down on the backlog. Often, it is really too early to get the team involved in any form of estimation. As you have stated, the CEO may ask you at some point if you are on track for a big release many sprints from today. Even if formal status is received through other channels in the organization, it is the Product Manager who is often associated with getting something done.

Additionally, while trying to maintain transparency, this can also have a few challenges. Some information might be very misleading to people further removed from the process. For instance, I have seen some sprints that failed which actually increased my confidence of a team's ability to deliver simply because the time was right, the team was close, and I knew that failing a sprint is exactly what the team needed at that time to get better. Yet to outsiders, a failed sprint seems to sound negative or even alarming.

—Michael Faisst

Michael's story nicely wraps up this chapter. He is sharing on a common theme from the Product Owner perspective, that it's a broad role, with incredible nuance and daily challenges.

Wrapping Up

❖ Many people underestimate the required breadth of the Product Owner role which then lessens its effectiveness. Don't do that! Instead consider these 4 functional areas: Product Manager, Project Manager, Leader, and Business Analyst as indicative of the roles breadth, depth, and skill challenges.

❖ While it IS about creating a product backlog for your team; don't fall into the trap of thinking that's ALL you do!

❖ As Michael's story illustrated, the Product Owner role is a conflicted one. Partly focused towards your team, yet also focused towards executives and important stakeholders. And let's not forget the customer in this. The expectation is that you're closely coupled to their needs and the value they seek.

It's easy to be pulled in multiple directions; becoming comfortable with that dynamic AND leveraging your entire team to help you is a key to overall success.

Chapter 4

The Product Owner as Leader

One of the more misunderstood parts of the Product Owner role is that of team leadership. Whenever I instantiate Scrum within an organization, I try to establish the Scrum Master and the Product Owner as leadership roles within their teams. I know, I know, agile teams are self-directed, but I've found it helps for both of these roles to understand the fundamentals of *Servant Leadership* [14] and to truly engage in leading their teams—particularly, early on within their agile adoption.

A great Product Owner must have innate leadership abilities or, at least, be willing to work on improving them as they develop and grow within their roles. Beyond themselves, they need to establish a leadership *partnership* of sorts with their Scrum Masters.

Understanding Your Team

I've worked with some Product Owners who don't become intimate with their teams capabilities and capacity. In other words, they don't get to *know* their team. Instead, they often allow the insatiable demands of the business, for more features than the team is capable of, to transparently pass through them and become frustrated and/or overly demanding with their teams.

Keep in mind there's a huge difference in driving the team with *BHAG* [15] goals versus constantly and stubbornly demanding extra effort and work than is clearly feasible. The former is related to becoming more intimate with your teams capacity, but slightly pushing them to do more than they think is possible. The latter is Waterfall and traditional, command-and-control leadership at its worst.

---

[14] Robert K. Greenleaf initiated the Servant Leadership movement in 1964 inspired by his work at AT&T. He wrote widely on the subject and, to my way of thinking, is still the leading author on the subject. You hear his philosophy quoted widely in the agile management & leadership community.

[15] Big Hairy Audacious Goal; a "stretch" goal of sorts. I don't believe great Product Owners should be motivating their team with soft or easily achieved goals. They should inspire the team and having them require some extra effort is part of that inspiration.

Every Product Owner has a responsibility to become intimate with the capacity of their teams along the lines of understanding:

- What is their average velocity Sprint-over-Sprint?
- Who are the strongest team members?
- Who are the technical and thought leaders?
- Who are the weakest team members? In what areas (technically and softer skills)?
- From a complimentary skills perspective, what are the teams overall strengths and gaps?
- What do they 'like' to do vs. not like to do?
- And finally, what motivates the individuals and the team as a whole?

You should also reflect on the same factors for yourself and the Scrum Master. Then, after having all of this team and self-realization information, factor it into your *thinking* around product backlog organization, sprint planning, goal setting, and external collaboration with stakeholders to discuss the team's capabilities and capacities.

One compelling reason for all of this reflection is to foster the passion and creative energy of your team. Agile teams don't necessarily go faster than their traditional counterparts. Instead, one of the speed factors of agility is creatively and energetically solving customer problems, with solutions that are simple and creative. Only by getting to know your team, can you frame your backlog and create the inherent challenges that foster an environment where this culture *emerges* from within your team.

Fostering Transparency

One of the ongoing insights I have discovered from my agile team leadership journey is continually realizing the awesome power of transparency. It's something that cuts through all of the traditional Waterfall *management speak*, for example: "Let's get this project back on schedule".

Excuse me, but it was never ON schedule! Instead, it's exactly where it was supposed to be given the challenges and our investment. The key isn't holding to some arbitrary schedule. Instead, the focus should be on adjusting to discoveries as you narrow in on your goal or target, and on delivering the highest value features without quality compromises.

Part of transparency is sharing your team's activity with your stakeholders as a natural course of project events. Not via specialized status reports, but by communicating with them on a real-time basis, for example:

- Asking them to walk-around the team's work area reviewing visible backlogs, plans, burn-down charts, etc.
- Inviting them to attend daily stand-ups to genuinely listen to the team's efforts and progress.
- Inviting them to sprint planning or backlog grooming and estimation meetings.
- Ensuring that they are included in (and attend) as many sprint reviews as possible.

I've found that stakeholders can underestimate the value and opportunity of sprint reviews over time and, therefore, their attendance can wane. Nothing can be more dangerous to your team's transparency. Project state information in agile teams is most effectively shared via face-to-face interactions. As part of your role and planning for each review, ensure that you've invited, and have reinforced the value of stakeholder attendance. If they need to be there…get them there!

Share good news with them wherever and whenever possible. Many of us like to give more attention to the bad news, but try not to solely focus on the challenges. Share with them how hard the team is working to solve problems and overcoming obstacles, as well as, how creative and energetic they are in attacking risks. Share with them how much they're _getting done_ and/or how much more is getting done then they originally planned or anticipated.

Of course you'll want to disclose the challenges facing the team, but always in the light of early discovery and adjustment. Remember, by the time bad news is revealed in traditional teams, it's often too late to take corrective action and still hold onto your targets. In Scrum teams you'll be getting _discovery on a daily basis_. Get ready for it. You'll know what's right and what's wrong weeks or months before you'd have discovered it in a traditional project.

You'll also be closer to the root cause of each challenge, so your corrective actions are more discrete and targeted towards solutions. Help your team and, more importantly, your stakeholders to realize that this level of transparency, while perhaps frightening and overwhelming at times, is _much different and much better_ than their traditional experiences.

Finally, remember that your Scrum Master is your partner in this transparency endeavor, so please don't go it alone. You both should be planning to ensure that _all_ aspects of your team's and projects' progress is boldly available in real-time for analysis by everyone. Be an "open book" in everything you do and always be honest.

Championing Your Team

A huge part of becoming a great Product Owner is aligning with, and becoming an advocate for, your team. This doesn't come for free. Nor, does it happen overnight. It will take effort on your part to learn, understand, and grow to trust one another.

As I said earlier, the first step is to become familiar with your team; their strengths, weaknesses, personality types, etc. You'll want to spend some time during work, as well as, off-hour times socializing with, and getting to know each of them. _Breaking bread_ [16] is a wonderful way to establish a strong team bond. This is a critical step that will pay ongoing dividends from a teamwork and business value delivery perspective.

At every opportunity, you need to become a _Voice_ for your team. When they're winning—shout it out! When they need help with a project, work with the Scrum Master to go out and get it. When they've "_Leaped Tall Buildings in a Single Bound_", make sure everyone knows that relative to their capacity or capability, this team is "Rockin!"

Most importantly, if your team needs you, always support them. No matter what else is on your plate, you need to be there for them—delivering on all aspects of your role. This may mean you have to either delegate tasks to other team members to help out, or to say "no" to your manager concerning other product management tasks. Have the _courage_ [17] to do what is best for your team!

---

[16] Joel Spolsky in his _Joel on Software_ blog recommends having lunch each day with his teams as an approach to building teamwork and enhancing cross-team collaboration. I've seen this referenced elsewhere and seen it work powerfully in my own teams.

[17] If you skipped over the Introduction and first few chapters, you might want to go back there and read about the breadth of the Product Manager/Owner roles. If

Setting a Leadership Example

There are four areas that come to mind when I think of great Product Owners setting a solid leadership example within their teams:

Taking on Work

I love it when the Product Owner takes on tasks within a sprint. We handle these as we would with any team member—with visibility and movement towards getting the work done. Often, the work has dependencies to other team members, so this puts delivery pressure on the Product Owner.

While the role is truly different, being a good team player and member is about helping each other out. It's useful to actually look for opportunities whenever you can; I normally see them exist in the following areas:

- Doing extra work to refine and add color to backlog items.
- Working with team members on individual user stories; perhaps even signing up for specific tasks.
- Always being available to review stories and acceptance tests as they develop; quickly providing real-time feedback.
- Trying to have time where you sit with your team; better that it be full-time, but regular *office hours* work well too.
- Writing acceptance tests and performing informal functional testing.

Clearly you don't want to take on too much sprint work, but showing that you're willing and chipping in to help when the team needs it, goes a long way to setting a leadership example.

Keeping it in the Family

Perhaps it's just the teams I've been associated with over the past few years, but I've seen a pattern emerge from certain Product Owners. They speak poorly about their teams to executives and other stakeholders. They generally fall into this pattern when the team hasn't delivered to external expectations. Normally, these expectations are not driven by transparent team capacity, but instead by traditional management, demand-based thinking, expecting the team to deliver beyond their realistic capacity.

---

you're a Product Manager, there's typically an awful lot on your plate—so this can be a particularly challenging stance for you...

Another aspect of this pattern is that Product Owners don't share their pressure and insight with their teams. Instead, they silently operate as if everything is going well and communicate to their teams that they're quite satisfied with the ongoing progress. I'm guessing this has something to do with conflict avoidance or, perhaps, background and/or culture.

I can't tell you how disruptive this is. First, they're not being good teammates or operating effectively within their role. Secondly, they're not defending their team and speaking to the real challenges that are being faced. Finally, they are simply not fostering trust. Trust me—the team will be aware of it. Watch out for this pattern and always try to deal with your teams and your projects congruently, with open and honest 360° dialogue.

Challenge Your Team!

Great Product Owners also challenge their teams. The first place to do this is with sprint goals. I truly struggle when a Product Owner comes into a sprint planning meeting with a flat, simple, non-compelling goal. It means they have no excitement, drive or vision, for the sprint; yet they expect the team to energetically respond to the customers' needs.

Instead, try to bring in something that will get the team motivated and get their blood pumping. It should be demanding and should challenge the team's capabilities at every turn. The term *"Stretch Goal"* comes to mind often—in that it should S-T-R-E-T-C-H the team—enabling them to grow and excel.

Another way to think about it is that every sprint should feel somewhat uncomfortable to them. It should create tension, as well as, excitement! They should also feel just a little nervous, with success being uncertain. These are just a few examples of the team dynamics that compelling sprint goals create.

I've seen a pattern in sprint planning where the team will plan a sprint only up to their capacity. Everyone will take on 100% of what they think they can deliver and then stop. This isn't a bad practice at all, particularly when you consider most engineers' propensity to underestimate their work.

However, a better practice is to identify stretch stories for the sprint, task them out, and place the stories/tasks on the sprint board for the sprint. The team buys into them as *stretch items* for this sprint while everyone tries to accomplish the planned work, as well as the stretch items. In my experience, mature Scrum teams will get to and complete the stretch items…and beyond 80% of the time.

A Not so 'Challenging' Story

On one occasion, I attended a presentation that a Product Owner was making to a group of sales people. It was a quarterly presentation where he was relating development progress against his last few quarterly promises. In many cases, he was falling back on those promises and, as you can imagine, the sales force became frustrated with the bad news. They were mostly frustrated because they had to again go out and explain to customers that many of their sorely needed features were delayed again. The Product Owner tried to explain the difficulties to everyone, but in the end, everyone was discouraged with the general lack of perceived progress.

Please understand, the agile teams were executing well; very well in this case and delivering significant release-over-release value. It was just that external expectations were not being met. (*Are they ever?*) Unfortunately, they were not being <u>set</u> very effectively in this case either.

(*Which was another takeaway for my ongoing coaching of this Product Owner*)

I followed him back into his Scrum team over the next week or so and noticed that not one word of those challenging and frustrating conversations was being shared with them. This was such a waste! He was a part of the team and transparency needs to go both ways. The team <u>needed</u> to hear that there were problems and frustrations and to realize they were not meeting external expectations. They also needed to consider what parts they could each play to respond to those expectations—as a team.

In this case, I felt the Product Owner should have been much more transparent in sharing the good news as well as the bad. He should have also expressed the personal frustration he felt in translating the team's work towards meeting sales expectations. To me, this was a wasted opportunity in engaging his team in his adversity to see how they might respond.

Your Partner

Great Product Owners establish a partnership with their Scrum Masters. The two of you are effectively the central leadership influences within your team. Clearly, your role is _more externally focused_, while the role of the Scrum Master is _more team or internally focused_.

You should observe this partnership to distinguish how you both can serve and coach your team to greater performance. Explore how you can remove impediments that are blocking their efforts; jointly focusing your teams on producing technically excellent results, delivering ultra-high quality software, and working towards gaining effective teamwork and collaboration.

A word on impediments; they're not just needs from the team that are raised in the daily stand-up! The most important impediments are the more subtle ones that the Scrum Master and Product Owner observe from their team's behaviors and delivery patterns, including things like:

- Your team isn't collaborating effectively, for example, developers are throwing work "over the wall" to testers or the testers aren't embracing agile collaboration with you or the developers.

- You don't have sufficient time to be an effective Product Owner; or the Scrum Master isn't focused full-time on their team. In general, solid agile practice coaching and preparation is being ignored.

- Nobody is addressing under-performers and performance issues: technical skill (programming skill, automation skills, domain knowledge, deliverable quality, etc.) within the team.

- Addressing under performance and performance issues—soft skills (collaboration, teamwork, transparency, and attitude) across the team.

- Stakeholders are expecting too much; asking the wrong questions, for example: "Are you on schedule for 100% of the scope?"; so they clearly don't understand the agile mindset nor trade-off goals.

- Team attrition—lack of fun and fulfilling work; too much by-rote activity; addressing burnout—everyone working too hard.

- Significant quality issues – team compromising quality over scope/time; a general lack of adherence to good agile quality practices and missing or ignoring your done-ness and other criteria.

All of the above are simple examples of the kinds of impediments that I'd expect fully partnered and collaborating Scrum Masters and Product Owners to be coaching _and leading_ their teams through. I'm going to say something quite contentious here. I think the notion of _self-direction_, which is, of course, central to great agile teams, is something that doesn't occur by accident. I think it's something that's coached, coaxed, guided, fostered, exampled, and led by you and the Scrum Master along with your teams.

Story – The REAL Single Wring-able Neck

Incredibly often in my agile and scrum classes someone will ask about accountability. Their question is based in the traditional management and Waterfall context where, when things go wrong, there's always someone you can blame. Or someone who can first, explain the problem to you, and who is next responsible for fixing the problem.

Quite often that person is a Functional Manager. Even more often, they have the title of Project Manager. In either case, they are the leadership "attack dogs" for sorting things out, finding out whom to blame, and getting things "back on track".

So the question in agile teams is: now that we've "gone Agile" who is this person? Is it...the Scrum Master? The Product Owner? Because we need SOMEONE since they are the key to ownership and accountability on the part of the team. Aren't they?

At iContact we had the notion of 'Swooping' in our agile teams. In that, if something was perceived to be going badly, a functional manager would "swoop into" a team and try to figure out what was wrong so they could "fix it". Our Scrum Masters coined the term.

It turned out that the swooping was driven by senior leadership, as they were looking for that single neck in agile teams and assumed it was the functional manager.

It turns out that there is no such neck in agile teams. If you want to know who's accountable for a sprints' results...it's the TEAM.

So there is no singularly accountable person. Now, I do think there is team leadership; i.e., the Scrum Master and Product Owner. Again at iContact for example, if there was an issue in a team, I would also speak to the Scrum Master and Product Owner to get their take on the situation. What was the problem? What was the team doing to mitigate or solve it? And did they need any 'help'?

I would always ask my management team to engage their respective team Scrum Masters and Product Owners before 'swooping' in and micro-managing the teams. I found this to be quite effective, but it was very different than traditional interactions.

And Afterwards...Reflection

While the retrospective setup and facilitation is in the realm of the Scrum Master, as the Product Owner and team member, you owe it to yourself to fully participate in the retrospective. While this is always vital, it's particularly important if the sprint didn't go well or failed to meet your expectations.

The retrospective is the one venue for you to raise points and issues of concern, both good and bad, from your particular functional perspective. Usually, the retrospective is a private event; including only the team. For that reason, it's a good place for private and challenging conversations as a team member.

To be honest, I see too many Product Owners missing this opportunity to give feedback to their teams. They simply *go along for the ride* and avoid the difficult or meaningful conversations, seeming to prefer being perceived as a *nice guy or gal*. Nothing could be more wasteful.

As I will continue to emphasize in the book, agile transparency is in all directions. Your role as a Product Owner requires you to express to your team the reality of their performance as it relates to external expectations and business needs. It's also to effectively evaluate their results in delivering value to you as a representative of the business. Please don't miss your opportunity to provide congruent team feedback via the sprint retrospective.

An Ongoing Debate

There's been an ongoing debate amongst Certified Scrum Trainers & Coaches as to whether the Product Owner should attend the teams' retrospective. The underlying message is questioning whether they are a member of the team or not. The driver for the discussion is a pattern many of them have seen where Product Owners place too much business and personal pressure on the team in the retrospective; rather than focusing on continuous team improvement.

So the thought is to exclude them from it so that they don't disrupt the teams' focus. I'm guessing here, but the debate is about 50/50 for and against excluding them. I'm against it.

First, I like the model where the Product Owner IS an included member of the team. They engage, are accountable to, and collaborate with their team. It's a central theme in this book and to becoming a great Product Owner.

Second, as a team member, I want them to be involved in the retrospective. Yes, they have a different point of view and role. And yes, they might have a tendency to de-rail the meeting. But, that's why the Scrum Master is there as the facilitator and also their partner. To me, the positive influence that the Product Owner can have in partnering with the team in their continuous improvement journey is far outweighed by any dangers. But that's just me…

Wrapping Up

❖ Get to know the strengths and characteristics of your team; then leverage that knowledge in crafting backlog work that supports business needs while leveraging the teams' skills and strengths.

❖ Share your thoughts and challenges with your team. Bring them up to speed on business dynamics and the competitive landscape. Also share internal pressures. Be clear and honest with them. Push them to be their best and deliver towards these pressures.

❖ Engage with your team. Pitch in and help and lead by example. Truly partner with your Scrum Master and endeavor to be a Servant Leader—doing whatever it takes to support your team.

Chapter 5

Understanding How Your Role Influences Quality

Maintaining ongoing product or application quality is one of the central themes within the agile methods. I remember the keynote presentation that Robert, 'Uncle Bob', Martin gave at the Agile 2008 Conference. It was entitled *Quintessence*. In it, he lamented the need for a fifth addition to the Agile Manifesto that emphasized *Craftsmanship over Crap*[18]. The essence of the presentation was the need for a relentless focus on professionalism and craftsmanship on the part of every agile team member.

The point being that quality is the responsibility of every team member. That it shouldn't enter a developer's mind to deliver a component that hasn't been properly designed or unit tested. It shouldn't enter the tester's mind to skip over testing functions that have clear value to the customer. It also shouldn't enter a Product Owner's mind to blindly demand features from their team or to challenge their estimates and integrity. Furthermore, they shouldn't ask for hacked up features simply to meet a date.

The team is expected to maintain the integrity of their craftsmanship regardless of any force that drives them towards delivering crap. More so than you might imagine, great Product Owners play a fundamental role in this endeavor; we'll explore those aspects next.

---

[18] http://blog.objectmentor.com/articles/2008/08/14/quintessence-the-fifth-element-for-the-agile-manifesto . I found the entire Keynote to be a call to arms for a pattern I've seen in quite a few agile teams. Teams have been too long blaming 'them' for their own quality compromises and sprint failures. 'They' could be the Scrum Master, Product Owner, and clearly business stakeholders and executives. Bob made the point that each individual and the team as a whole are responsible for their work and their compromises. That if lines need to be held, they should be responsible and hold to them.

Let's Be Clear, You Don't Test In Quality

I spend a great deal of time coaching various teams in their agile adoption journeys and make this point in every introductory class. But, inevitably after we're done sprinting, I hear team members, cross-functional stakeholders, and executives talking about testing and quality as if they were synonymous.

Read my lips. *You don't test in quality*. By the time you get to testing, it's too late. Your quality has already been instantiated into your code. Instead, you build quality into your DNA and work habits by individually adopting some of these core values:

- Build quality into your stories by sitting down with actual customers and precisely understanding their challenges and usage.
- Make your product backlogs transparent and easily available to everyone. Encourage questions and feedback.
- Listen deeply to your stakeholders and understand their priorities and needs.
- Build quality into your code by collaborating and pairing while performing more formal code reviews whenever possible, particularly on the more complex sections or areas where you're in unfamiliar territory.
- If you encounter some horrible pre-existing code hacks, consistently endeavor to re-factor and improve or simplify them. Always leave the code better "after you're gone".
- Take the time to create thoughtful tests at every level (unit, feature, system, regression) and then relentlessly test as early as possible.
- Automate all tests so you can run them quickly, achieving continuous feedback for ongoing changes.
- If you do decide to 'skip' work at any level, place it on the backlog for future clean-up and improvement. Make the trade-off transparent and commit to doing it.
- Never blame management, or others, for the lack of quality. Instead, as part of your team, professionally hold yourself accountable to the highest principles and standards.

Aspects of Quality

So, what did the previous list imply? Hopefully, the implication was that quality does not equal testing. While testing IS an important part of the equation, it is certainly not all of it.

As you define your product backlog, you are building quality into the system. Every debate that you have within your team concerning requirements, how to implement them and how to make them simpler and more directed towards the customers' needs, will improve your quality.

Every session you have where you engage with customers to truly understand their business and operational needs, will improve the quality of the requirements. You do this, not only for your customer, but to improve the quality of the requirements presented to your team.

Within the software development process itself, there are critical quality points. The early emphasis points include architecture, design collaboration, and inspection. At times, it appears as if the Agile Methodologies don't sufficiently stress good software design. By the time you reach the system level, component level, and individual feature level, the team should be engaged in collaborative design and team reviews. Even as they increment the design, this should be happening in thin slices of end-to-end behavior. Everyone should understand and be able to follow the overall system design.

Another critical quality step is code reviews and/or inspections. A big part of XP's Pair Programming practice is focused towards inspection-like activity, acknowledging that two sets of eyes are better than one. The other important aspect in reviews is catching errors or bugs early, when they are the easiest and cheapest to resolve.

Testing is still a quality practice, simply not the only one. Within most agile teams, I've noticed a narrowing in the testing focus. It's typically driven from the unit, story acceptance, and story functionality perspectives. This, more or less, ensures that the backlog deliverables are working.

However, there is much more to testing than simply qualifying the individual features. Later on in this chapter, I'll try to expand the definition of testing so that you consider its broadly nuanced depth and breadth. This should help ensure your backlogs enable sufficient testing during each sprint and, more importantly, for your releases.

Finally, agile Continuous Integration (CI) and automated testing practices provide the safety-net that is needed to be able to make small, fast system changes or extensions, while getting real-time feedback. Many think that their focus should be on speed. Actually, the automation investment in the agile methods is related to feedback, since we're trying to make those small incremental changes as quickly and as safely as possible.

Always driving quality before speed!

Traditional & Agile Quality Practices

The assumption is often made by many people outside the agile community that the methods are not a quality play. The reality is quite the opposite. Many of the practices do not resemble their Waterfall equivalents. Figure 1, lists the traditional quality practices and tries to correlate them to their agile counterparts.

This list isn't necessarily complete, but it does give you a sense for the type of quality practices that should be occurring within your Scrum teams. And as a part of your role, you need to foster, support, and lead these activities as much as possible.

Traditional Quality Approaches or Practices	Agile Practices with a Similar Focus
Requirement Gathering	Conducting user story writing workshops and collaborative product backlog construction
Requirement Qualification	Running sprint reviews with customers present; adapting to feedback with reduced change cost
Code Inspection or Reviews	Pair Programming; Pair Testing; using collaborative tools for distributed reviews
Code Quality	TDD or Unit Testing practices; Pairing developers and testers
Quality Control, process-driven practices, checklists, repositories,	Applying Lean practices in software development; emphasizing Professionalism & Craftsmanship within the team
Configuration Management Processes	Continuous Integration as a practice; fixing broken builds in a stop-the-line

Traditional Quality Approaches or Practices	Agile Practices with a Similar Focus
	fashion; transparency
Risk Management practices	Iteratively inspecting results; raising risks and immediately dealing with them within the team
Plan documents (Project, Test, Documentation, Development, Overall); Project Schedules	Minimal planning – overlay the backlog via release planning; face-to-face communication on steps; Scrum of Scrums for dependency coordination
Requirement Traceability	Numbering stories and acceptance tests; keeping track of pass/fail rates per user story
Project and other status reporting	Transparency; Wiki's, Burndowns, maintaining other Information Radiators in the team room
Defect Triage; Change Control Boards	Fixing defects individually—at the most responsible moment; deferring few bugs
Architecture and Design Reviews	Incremental or emergent practices—delivering features as end-to-end, thin slices of functionality; simply, metaphors for system architecture and flow

Figure 1, Examples of Traditional Quality Practices and their Agile Counterparts

Next, I want to discuss the role that the great Product Owner has in collaborating with team members—without negatively influencing their work quality.

Don't Push Compromise—Instead Trust

As a Product Owner, you have to walk a fine line between asking your teams to explain and quantify their quality decisions, yet not push them too hard and thus drive quality compromises into their work.

In the first edition of *Extreme Programming* by Kent Beck, he drew a clear and stark distinction between the role of the customer (Product Owner) and the role of the team. In it, he emphasized that the customer drove work prioritization, scope trade-off decisions, and then finally, accepted the team's work.

But Beck emphasized that teams made the technical decisions surrounding architecture and design. Ultimately, while you can explore various design aspects with the team and discuss trade-offs, once it was decided _what was wanted/needed,_ they were responsible for _how it was to be implemented_. They were also responsible for _how long it would take_. He also reminded us that good agile customers always kept in mind that team estimates were even more sacrosanct than their designs.

This stark delineation came out of respect for each of our professional experience and roles. Kent alluded to the team's need to respect and value the customer role within the team. Yes, debate scope definition and data requirements; however, in the end, the customer is accountable for driving business value so, listen to them.

The reciprocal is trusting in your team. If they say a component needs refactoring, they mean it. If they say it will take five days to complete a section of work, even when you only feel it should only take a day, trust them. Remember, they are experienced professionals, members of your team, and they're the ones who will be doing the work!

The following two stories illustrate the responsibility and importance of effective influence and trust within agile teams.

A Story of Influence

On one occasion, I was the Scrum Master for a team that struggled with a series of sprints. We had committed to certain work being done but, in one particular sprint, we missed our goals badly. In our retrospective, it surfaced that team members had grossly underestimated the complexity and scope of a series of stories which made up the core of the sprint.

I remember the planning meeting dynamics, but didn't recall observing a problem in the planning. When questioned, the team said that the Product Owner had influenced them to cut their estimates because of the importance of the work. Again, I didn't remember the meeting having that sort of dynamic and pushed the team for more information. After some time, they admitted that the Product Owner had not 'made' them do anything. Based on their perception of external pressures, they had decided to be highly optimistic and only consider the sunny day paths in their estimates and subsequent work. OF COURSE, that wasn't the case and the work, took much longer than expected to deliver.

In defense of the team, this particular Product Owner had a style where he would always push his team(s) for shorter timeframes in their estimates; whether that was in product backlog grooming, or sprint planning meetings. He wasn't malicious, but would always speak of the customers' desperate need for a particular feature, or mention the pressure he was getting from the CEO. There was always some sort of crisis and he would constantly let the team know about it.

Based on this behavior and his close relationship with the team, he could easily cause the team to totally unravel when it came to understanding, planning, collaborating and delivering good work. It turned out to be a case of good engineering vs. hacking and, much of the time; they felt influenced to 'hack' in order to make their Product Owner 'happy'. Unfortunately, this wasn't the sole doing of the Product Owner. It was also part of the team dynamic and the team was certainly a partner in this dance!

Of course the trade-offs, more often than not, resulted in software issues that the Product Owner had to explain to the customers anyway. So in their efforts to do 'more', they actually did less.

In order to change this pattern, the Product Owner began to strongly emphasize the design and overall feature quality in all interactions with the team; always over-emphasizing its importance. Rather quickly, the team began to change the nature of its deliverables and was even able to entertain healthy quality level trade-off discussions without resorting to their prior hacking behaviors.

A Story of Strong Arming

I was recently consulting with a team on an "agile project" where they had made an entire set of up-front estimates for all features required within the project. They were part of a larger-scale Waterfall environment, so up-front requirement analysis, high level design, and schedule commitments were necessary to gain financial approval for ANY project.

Once their Director saw the estimates consolidated into the schedule, she was livid that it didn't align with business expectations. In order to ensure that the schedule was aggressive, she invited every engineer on the team into her office and went through their estimates—line by line. In addition, she challenged them face-to-face and questioned why their estimates couldn't be reduced.

To make a long story short, each engineer crumbled under the pressure. They basically agreed with whatever the Director thought were the correct estimates and then moved on. Once the entire schedule was miraculously shortened by 30%, the Director was 'happy' and the team promptly began working. Over a period of time, however, the project started to encounter problems. Since the engineers were sprinting in their deliveries, issues surfaced more quickly. However, it soon became glaringly evident that the team had underestimated the work.

A couple of problems occurred before they delivered their project. Because of schedule demands, the developers started reducing their quality practices (unit tests, pairing, Cucumber tests, and inspections). Instead, they put more demands on the testers to find issues in test—simply throwing it over the wall and, clearly, reverting to Waterfall behaviors.

The job also took about 35% more time, which meant that their original estimates, Waterfall or agile-based, closely represented their original estimates. When they finally released the product, they found (actually their customers found) many more defects than anticipated; this created even more rework time. In fact, product stability is still their primary challenge today and it all relates back to their quality versus time decision-making.

The Director in this story didn't trust her team and took the wrong path of strong-arming them into reducing their work estimates. I've been working with software development teams for 25 years and believe this is one of the most absurd things you can do.

Early on in any/every software project, things are ill defined. Engineers simply don't know the future. Anyone in a position of authority can come in and easily influence them to cut down their plans.

The results of this, however, ripple through the project and the team. It doesn't, and won't, build confidence or trust. The team doesn't self-organize. They also don't take ownership of their own incremental improvement.

As a great Product Owner, you shouldn't strong-arm or overly influence your teams. Yes, explain the business challenges. Yes, engage in healthy debate and challenge their designs, approaches, estimates, and work. But in the end, trust their craftsmanship and professionalism by not pushing too hard. If you do, they will succumb and you will ALL lose!

Traditional Testers in Agile Teams

It's often the case that traditional testers struggle in their role transformation from Waterfall to agile methods. In traditional teams their role is very much at the end of the pipeline. Sure, they have some early planning and preparation to do but, in the end, developers throw software "over the wall" to them for testing. Typically, the development team is over schedule and there is always compression of testing plans and time. There is usually little cross-team collaboration and often they are blamed for overall application quality, even though they play only a part in that regard.

In agile teams, the dynamic fundamentally changes. Instead of being at the end, testers need to move to the beginning of the process. They actually become your partner in defining and refining user stories. Not only in crafting the story definitions, but where testers can really shine, is in the areas of well-formed and comprehensive acceptance tests.

Their primary and up-front role becomes, more or less, a Business Analyst one where they serve as a liaison between you and the development team; refining stories and ensuring their quality execution. They should be partners with development, often pairing with them, to assure that feature development is clear and aligned with the customers' needs.

Another part of their role transformation surrounds that of a quality advocate or the "Voice of Quality". Many traditional testers are placed in the role of 'gatekeeper', ensuring that quality goals are held within the release. However, they are rarely afforded the responsibility or time to do this effectively. In agile teams there is a holistic focus on quality, yet the team can lack some of the core experience to achieve their goals. Good testers can really help their teams here as well by keeping their focus on up-front quality versus attempts to test it in.

In essence, agile testers move from the end of the development pipeline to become the upfront _Quality Champions_ within their agile teams. Their final focus is on relentless test automation. Not by doing it themselves, but by influencing their entire team (and you as the Product Owner) to invest in test automation.

The Breadth of Testing

Now that I've harped so much on your "quality mindset", I think we ought to explore some of the dynamics of traditional testing. Testing is one of the most misunderstood aspects of solid agile development, particularly as it scales. Software testing is so much more than simply unit, functional, or regression testing. In iterative methodologies, one of the great challenges is not over or under testing, but hitting the right amount of coverage given the specific amount of code changed (added, removed, and changed) within each iteration.

The other balancing act is to test as early as possible. For example, if you're constructing a web application, quite often performance is a key concern. While you might design with performance in mind, you often need to test the performance dynamics of the application to fully understand everything. So, there is always pressure to perform some early benchmarking and performance testing.

However, there's a Catch-22 here. Often you need the majority of the application to be architecturally sound before performance testing is possible or, at least, valuable and informative. This very fact can drive testing too late in the development process or, possibly too late to do anything constructive with the feedback. Performance testing is just one of the testing activities that come into play this way.

As you can see in Figure 2, there is a wide range of testing practices that might be required for your project. It also illustrates the typically narrow focus of agile testing versus the breadth that is required for most projects. Plus, at the bottom, it lists some of the non-functional requirement testing activities that, again, extend our views beyond typical agile testing. Clearly, agile testing is not a black box activity.

As a great Product Owner, you need to have a firm understanding of the nuance and breadth of testing that is required to create robust products that delight your customers. Partner with your testers and genuinely listen to their advice regarding when, where, and how much to test during your iterations. They can also provide advice [19] for effectively planning release-level testing, which is usually much broader than its sprint-level counterpart.

Strong Focus – Agile Team Testing		Weak Focus – Agile Team Testing		
• Unit Testing • Automated Builds – Smoke Testing • Focused – Customer Acceptance Testing		• Integration Testing • Functional Testing • System Testing • Regression Testing • Performance Testing • Load Testing		
Moderate Focus – Agile Team Testing		Often Forgotten Testing Activities in Agile Contexts		
• Test Driven Development (TDD) • Very limited – Integration & Regression Testing • Focused Towards Automation • Limited Exploratory Testing		• Scenario Based Testing • User Acceptance Testing (UAT) • Usability Testing, Other Non-functional Testing (*see below*) • Exploratory Testing • Large-scale Automation		
Examples of Non-Functional Testing Types				
• Availability, Efficiency, Flexibility, Integrity, Interoperability • Maintainability, Portability, Reliability, Reusability • Robustness, Testability, Usability, Performance, Security				

Figure 2, Agile Testing Focus and Non-functional Testing Activities

Technical & Test Debt

One important idea the agile movement has surfaced is the notion of *technical debt*. If you've been developing software for any length of time, you've experienced technical debt; although you may not have realized there was a term coined for it. Technical debt surrounds the idea that software, virtually any software, gets more brittle over time. It ages. As different people work on it, it gets more and more complex, harder to understand, and even harder to maintain.

---

[19] One of my reviewers, Craig McCrary suggested that I put a glossary in the book that explained technical terms; particularly some of the nuance behind the testing terms in Figure 2. If you find that you don't understand any aspect of testing, I recommend that you "talk to your testers". They can explain general terminology AND how they're uniquely applying testing approaches in your projects.

There are only two effective strategies for dealing with technical debt. First, is to let your software age and not really invest much in its maintenance. Over time, it becomes harder to maintain and more riddled with bugs. At some point, you get tired of the risk and you either retire the application or you decide to re-architect a replacement. In either case, you're making a "Big Bang" decision regarding the technical debt.

The agile methodologies have come up with a different strategy for handling the debt.

Instead of letting it accrue and get larger, what if you worked at reducing it in small steps? Suppose you try and release software with fewer bugs and then fix new bugs as soon as possible. What would happen if and when you discover a section of the code that is poorly designed, you re-design (refactor) it right then and there? This continuous improvement strategy aligns perfectly with the Agile Manifesto and is probably the better way to attack technical debt—in small, one optimization at a time, steps.

This same idea can be applied to the testing space and to both manual and automated test cases. In fact, I also think there is a notion of Technical Test Debt in most agile projects; particularly those that can't test everything within the sprint. Whenever you move onto producing more software without performing all of your tests, you're introducing test debt in the form of untested areas of the application.

How do you compensate for these two forms of debt? As we'll explore in Chapter 16, you test it out via hardening iterations that focus on integration, regression, and non-functional testing.

Wrapping Up

❖ The major intent of this chapter was to broaden your awareness of the breadth, depth, and importance of testing within iterative methods. It's not simple; usually because not all testing can be performed within each sprint.

❖ The other key point was to encourage and influence you to partner with the testers on your teams and within your organization. Ask them to help you in refining your backlog so that quality and testing is appropriately represented at a sprint and release level.

❖ Literally, the Product Backlog needs to represent the focus of traditional Quality and Test plans and their strategies for delivering high-quality and robust software.

Section 2

Product Backlogs

There are five chapters in this section focused towards the dynamics of creating and maintaining a healthy product backlog for your teams. The central focus in this section is the individual product backlog feeding a single Scrum team. There's a bit of a "chicken and egg" challenge in this chapter discussing backlogs, stories, themes, etc. in a linear flow. So, I might have some cross-references you need to follow if you are totally new to Scrum. I hope you don't find that too confusing.

Chapter 6 – A View of the Product Backlog
Here we explore the basic definition and view to what a Product Backlog is, and how the Product Owner needs to establish and guide it.

Chapter 7 – 'Grooming' the Product Backlog
Once you have a backlog, remember that it's an organic construct that is continuously being modified. It's part requirement list; but more than that, it's the game plan for the each teams release workflow.

Chapter 8 – Creating the Product Backlog
I often get asked, but where do stories "come from?" My common answers include: from the Product Owner, from the Team, and from a Story Brainstorming Workshop. I find variations of the latter to be very effective at creating or updating backlogs.

Chapter 9 – Writing User Stories
User stories have become the de facto standard for representing agile requirements. They have some interesting qualities and can be challenging to "get right". While the Product Owner doesn't have to write every story, you should be able to discern good from bad.

Chapter 10 – Managing the Initial Product Backlog
We explore where backlogs and stories "come from" and how to instantiate your backlog from scratch. Valuation, prioritization, and thematic composition are important parts of the organization.

Chapter 6

A View of the Product Backlog

Great Product Owners essentially _own_ the product backlog. To quote one of my Product Owner friends, it's like "table stakes" for the role. They understand how important a well-crafted backlog is. They understand the nuance of now versus later items and creating value and momentum. They understand how it maps to phased or iterative project delivery points. They fully understand that, while it is just a _simple list_, it's much more than that too.

It's important to define or, depending on your understanding of Scrum, re-define the nature of the product backlog. From my perspective the product backlog is:

> "A Product Backlog is simply a prioritized list of all work that the team needs to complete in order to deliver on the vision and promise of a product or project. It's composed of Product Backlog Items, or PBI's, which are succinct units of functionality or work, with priority implying delivery timing along with business and technical value."

For an alternate perspective, the _Scrum Alliance_[20] defines it this way:

> "The product backlog (or "backlog") is the requirements for a system, expressed as a prioritized list of product backlog items. These include both functional and _non-functional_[21] customer requirements, as well as technical team-generated requirements[22]"

---

[20] www.scrumalliance.com – sort of the Scrum governing board, although it's primarily driven by Ken Schwaber.

[21] Non-functional requirements cover non feature driven areas. They are often referred to as the 'ILITIES', in that examples include—Maintainability, Reliability, Usability, and Supportability. Quite often Security and Performance requirements are included as well.

[22] So here I could envision frameworks and architecture, refactoring or redesign recommendations, packages of bug fixes, and testing or infrastructural work as common examples of _other_ work.

And finally, here's the description in the *Scrum Guide*[23]:

> The Product Backlog is an ordered list of everything that might be needed in the product and is the single source of requirements for any changes to be made to the product. The Product Owner is responsible for the Product Backlog, including its content, availability, and ordering.
>
> A Product Backlog is never complete. The earliest development of it only lays out the initially known and best-understood requirements. The Product Backlog evolves as the product and the environment in which it will be used evolves. The Product Backlog is dynamic; it constantly changes to identify what the product needs to be appropriate, competitive, and useful. As long as a product exists, its Product Backlog also exists.
>
> The Product Backlog lists all features, functions, requirements, enhancements, and fixes that constitute the changes to be made to the product in future releases. Product Backlog items have the attributes of a description, order, and estimate.

Notice that I mention _all work_, as well as, feature and functionality items, which goes slightly beyond the Scrum Alliance and Scrum.org / Scrum Guide definitions. I'm somewhat a stickler for including all of the teams work items within the backlog. So, if an aspect of a product or project costs something to deliver, I believe it needs to be _visible_ on the backlog!

For example, the following user story:

> Acquiring performance testing software and installing / configuring it for team Use ...

...should be a Product Backlog Item on your Backlog.

---

[23] Scrum Guide, October 2011 version, except from page 12
http://www.scrum.org/Scrum-Guides

I would argue that it's more of a task than a feature, but it still belongs there. As do these stories:

> Performing regression testing to meet regulatory coverage goals of 95% or

> Meet with operations team to plan and script release deployment steps.

Product Backlog Items

In the purest sense of Scrum, as it was initially defined, the Product Backlog Item's or PBI's were simple entries in an Excel spreadsheet that defined requirements and/or work that needed to be completed by the team. Usually they were a statement of, at most, a sentence or two. There was little time spent defining the specific format of a PBI or, what constituted a *good* PBI, as that was purely left to the implementer of Scrum to do with their team and within business contexts.

Nonetheless, most early Scrum teams used spreadsheets for their backlogs. The concept of a user story then surfaced as a development practice within the XP (Extreme Programming) community. User stories are requirement artifacts that are quite lightweight; we'll explore them in more detail in Chapters 8 & 9. However, from my perspective, they've become the de facto standard for defining PBI's within Scrum and XP teams.

That doesn't mean that they're the only method. You can still have PBI's that connect to other requirement formats, i.e., agile use cases or traditional requirement specifications. Also, in some Scrum teams, the original 1-2 sentence guidance is still used as the sole requirement definition for the team.

For the purposes of this book, I'm going to focus on the user story as the central representation of a Scrum PBI. I just don't want you to feel it's the only one. My main reason for this focus is the *behaviors* that user story reinforce surrounding solid agile requirement practices. So, even if you're not using stories, you should still find useful advice in these discussions.

For example, combined with the user story is the notion of *acceptance tests*. These are verifiable statements that support the base behavior of the story.

They contain the Product Owners direction as to what aspects of the requirements are crucial; needing to be verified prior to accepting the story. Clearly, this notion can be applied to agile use cases and any other form of agile requirements artifact.

Next, I want to share a short story related to prioritization. Sometimes we trivialize the effort it takes to truly create a well-ordered (prioritized) backlog. It can actually be quite challenging in practice.

Mike's Story – Backlog Prioritization

I want to stress the difficulty of prioritization within Scrum teams. In my opinion, this is the most demanding aspect of an Agile Product Owner.

As Scrum Master, I attended a sprint planning meeting recently where all backlog items were marked "Priority 1". (I'm not kidding!) When I questioned the Product Owner about this, his answer was "Well, we need them all." He happened to be new to Scrum. I was disappointed that in my previous training he failed to grasp the important point that a Product Backlog needs to be clearly and uniquely prioritized.

I immediately postponed the Sprint Planning meeting due to un-prioritized backlog items. I then spent more time mentoring the Product Owner on how to prioritize and make necessary tradeoffs, to realize why this was important, and to understand the fact that prioritization is, in general, a very difficult endeavor. But, it does need to be done for the sake of the project. It takes a lot of hard work and thought to set priorities that are optimal to help the project become successful.

After this additional round of coaching, the rescheduled Sprint Planning meeting went a whole lot smoother.

—Mike Hall

The key point that Mike makes is that backlog prioritization is really demanding. It takes effort, commitment and a lot of hard work. It also never stops. I hope that the back-story here is that Mike as the Scrum Master and his Product Owner used this as a springboard to their partnership and collaboration.

Another View to the Backlog

Another way I like to think of the product backlog is as a serial project plan or Gantt chart. I know this is contrary to a lot of agile pundit thinking, but it's true. The backlog sequencing should have a significant connection to traditional software project workflows, for example:

- For complex or large projects, you should still be able to see some architecture definition and design phasing early within the backlogs' workflow; clearly early on, and intermittently, as the design emerges.

- When approaching a planned release point, you should see the testing of maturing features leading toward the release; as well as, inclusion of other functional work (for example: documentation, training, operational readiness, and release steps).

- You should see riskier items being surfaced, developed, and tested earlier. In fact, risk mitigation becomes a central theme surrounding what you take on and when, within the backlogs' workflow.

- If the team is unclear about major and minor work items, you should see references to research-oriented sprints or user stories (story - research spikes) interleaved throughout the backlog.

- You should also see the team *actively* contributing to refactoring items; testing automation items; defining architectural and design items; reworking of items, and getting together packages of meaningful, high-impact bug repairs, etc. within the backlog.

The key point here is that there should be a great deal of execution nuance described within your product backlog; so endeavor to view it in that way.

A Tapestry

For the past 2-3 years, I've been using a tapestry metaphor in my Product Ownership classes. I've found it useful to illustrate the nuanced breadth of a healthy and balanced backlog.

For any backlog, I want to view it linearly and look for 'threads' that represent more global activities or concerns. For example, if the team is working on a new project, I'll look for architecture and design threads throughout the backlog. I'll ask questions like:

- Are there architecturally focused stories in the backlog? And design activities?
- Where are they located? Are they more front-end or back-end loaded?
- Are designs being done at all? Are they being reviewed at appropriate phases? Or documented?
- Are there enough story research spikes being planned? (I look for something along the lines of 10-20% of the overall functional stories)
- When does architecture and design stabilize? Relative to the release target?

This is not intended to be an exhaustive list. The point really is to examine your backlog along multiple perspectives (threads) to enhance the overall quality of its contents and structure.

Figure 3, contains more ideas for threads that you should be looking for in your own backlogs; from my perspective, the more thread-driven analysis you have, the better.

Backlog 'Threads'	
✓ Features & Themes	✓ Deployment
✓ Value Increments	✓ Regulatory
✓ Architecture	✓ Dependencies
✓ Design	✓ Risk
✓ Process	✓ Feedback
✓ Quality	✓ Customer Timing
✓ Functional Testing	✓ Release Tempo
✓ Non-Functional Testing	✓ Documentation

Figure 3, Backlog Tapestry 'Threads'

Partitioning the Backlog

I like to equate projects and methodologies towards the phasing within a chess match. I don't play a lot of chess, but I do understand the distinction between opening moves, middle game and end game and how they 'partition' the thinking around the various phases of the game. You can similarly apply these same workflow characteristics to software projects.

From a software perspective:

- **Opening Moves:** Are focused towards initial or setup steps in your project. For example, clarifying requirements, doing some iterative design, sorting out initial architecture, and/or planning refactoring needs as you move forward. Other start-up work such as forming or re-forming a team and gathering environments (tools, space, systems, etc.) are all opening move activities.

  Key focus: Emergent architecture and design, exploration, understanding and clarity.

- **Middle Game:** Is primarily focused towards construction of features and value for the project. In an agile context, this means delivering fully tested *packages or theme*s of features. It also means that ongoing refactoring and overall rework is being performed, as the design emerges.

  Key focus: Creating functional mass, quality, stability, maintaining simplicity, and delivering value.

- **End Game:** Is normally focused towards delivery. In an agile context, this means more traditional testing and general product maturation. It also means cross-functional readiness across the entire organization—everyone getting ready to deploy, support, and sell the new version of the product or application.

  Key focus: Stabilization testing, code freeze, quality, product integration, and deployment readiness.

This is another way to assess the health and maturity of your backlog. Overlay it with these three phases and look for expected activities associated with each. Quite often you'll find missing items by taking this phased review approach.

If you're interested in seeing this concept in practice, you might want to skip ahead to Chapter 16 and the discussion of the Agile Release Train, which serves as a good example of the phasing I'm suggesting here.

Backlog Length – Does it Matter?

There is a good deal of debate over the size of the *typical* product backlog. From the lean community, you'll hear a great deal of advice around keeping it short. There is good reason for this. As you move down within the backlog, out in time if you will, one could argue that any investment in writing details down, and spending time substantially discussing stories, is wasteful.

That *waste*[24] is from a lean perspective where you don't want to invest much time in things that might change drastically and that don't provide immediate value to your customer. Instead it's much wiser to defer work to

---

[24] You'll also hear waste referred to as *Muda* in the Lean community.

the last responsible moment, and then do just enough work to meet their (and your) needs.

There are other camps who think that having a list which represents all requirements for a particular product or project can be helpful. Mostly because they feel it captures and illustrates the overall business expectations and scope. In this case, the thinking goes that you invest very little on the lower level items so, why not keep them around. They can provide insights to the team and stakeholders regarding overall vision, as well as longer term needs for the project. It also can have a sobering effect in that it influences scope reductions and adjustments by your stakeholders; simply as a reaction to the sheer size of the list.

I've seen both 'sides' work effectively, but lean (pun intended), towards the latter camp. I don't think it hurts to have an exhaustive backlog, as long as you maintain your composure about investing in its development. You also never know when items in the backlog may spark some creative solution or stakeholder insight that can truly change the game. From my perspective, it's a fairly low investment, low fidelity mind-map that has a lot of visionary value for the team.

A potential negative side-effect of this approach is demoralizing your team, or your stakeholders for that matter, with the sheer scope of the project. So, ensure that this isn't happening if you lean towards the latter approach. Here's a personal rule of thumb, or heuristic, for backlog attention to detail:

- **Short Term:** You'll need 3-4 Sprints worth of details in your product backlog leading to your next planned project or product release point. This is your short term clarity around your current release commitment.

  Typically what drives the amount of these PBI's is your release model, or how many sprints encompass your typical release point. The more sprints the more backlog items.

- **Medium Term:** Next is perhaps another 3-6 Sprints of medium to high level PBI's. Invest minimally in these items or stories. Size them roughly. Keep them short and simple. Perhaps cluster the items into packages or themes so that the team can better understand the direction they'll be heading.

These won't be large-scale epics, as they're targeted for the next release. But they will be large, sprint executable stories. When you're grooming the medium-term, you are preparing for your next release plan.

- **Longer term:** Beyond this point, throw in whatever you've got on the list! Try to keep it in approximate, or rough, priority order. Invest ever so slightly in item clarity; although it's better to have the items at a high level (Epics) throughout.

These are your true, larger scope epics. These stories clearly aren't executable within a sprint. They vary in size and in many cases, need story research spikes to explore their complexity.

These are also the stories that revolve around the far-flung future; something I call Future-Cast that I explore later on in this chapter.

Lucy's Story – A Rather Sizable Backlog

I was working with a Product Owner at iContact by the name of Lucy. Lucy was a relatively new Product Owner, having been newly hired into the role. She had solid domain experience and immediately created a healthy rapport with her team.

After several months in the role, I happened to have a hallway chat with Lucy regarding her backlog. It went something like this:

I asked Lucy about her backlog grooming and generally how it was going. She proudly claimed that she had groomed about 500 points worth of user stories with her team. They were all finely grained and execution ready. She was obviously incredibly pleased with how much work she and the team had put into this well-crafted backlog.

I was a bit taken aback though. I knew most of our team's velocity to be around 25 points for a two-week sprint. In the back of my mind I was doing the math around how much of a backlog Lucy and the team had groomed. It turned out that she and the team had about a year's worth of backlog "in the bag". At our current quarterly release tempo, they had presumed to plan out in short-term detail, 4 releases of work. And they were still grooming...

At the risk of demoralizing Lucy, I had to tell her that I thought she might have been a bit overzealous in grooming. Particularly since, as an organization, we rarely could decide on our products' focus 1-2 releases in advance. I tried to gently convince her to throttle a bit back on her grooming intensity and to allow some of the stories to be 'larger', while deferring much of the grooming.

While I valued Lucy's initiative, her focus was wrong in a couple of ways. First, she had groomed all of her stories at the same, short-term level. By the way, this took a lot of effort for her and the team to decompose and scope all the stories at that level. Second, she had clearly groomed too many stories too far in advance. And the final mistake she made was not leveraging the multi-level granularity approach that allows the team to look down the road with larger stories and epics; as you'll see in future-cast section below.

20/30/50 Rule

Finally, here's another sizing heuristic you might find helpful, it's the 20/30/50 rule as *I 'heard' it expressed in the Scrum discussion groups*[25]. I think this is close to my own views regarding effective backlog balance, but perhaps is a bit more succinct and useful view. It follows that a well-balanced backlog is:

- 20% proper stories ready to roll; execution ready in the next sprint or two
- 30% are larger (8-13-20 point) stories or epic stories that will eventually be split out into smaller finely grained ones; targeted for the next release point
- 50% are large epics or themes—vague ideas about long term product direction. I never put much effort here because it's almost always wrong.

Alternative View – 2 Work Backlogs, 1 Workflow

I have seen other teams take on a different view to their backlogs. Their experience implies that having the all the tasks; technical, process, quality, and infrastructural work *mixed up with* the product features, muddies the

---

[25] I noticed this in an exchange authored by Mark Levison on November 12, 2008 in the Scrumdevelopment Yahoo Group.

value focus of the backlog. They actually prefer having two separate product backlogs per team.

One backlog, as alluded to, is solely focused towards the feature set for their product or project. Everything on the list has clear business value and is a visible part of their application. The other backlog contains virtually everything else; for example: bug repairs, refactoring work, setting up team development or testing infrastructure, establishing testing frameworks, testing or process steps, and managing dependencies with other teams.

The proponents of this approach are driven by a desire for improved _focus_. They, and their business stakeholders, are focused much more so on the _Feature-Based Backlog_, while the _Additional-Work Backlog_ is more in the realm of the entire team and much more focused towards the technical, quality, and delivery aspects for the application.

My major issue with this approach is losing the transparency of interrelated backlog items and their dependencies and/or relationships. I prefer the idea of encouraging the 'Business' to consider all work in an effort to remain _balanced_ in their decision-making. Clearly, in this scenario, they'll focus on the feature-based backlog when selecting sprint candidate work. However, you may run the risk of them getting a pass on the additional-work backlog.

If you can truly influence your business stakeholders to balance between the two lists in determining the appropriate priority and workflow, then I think having multiple lists might work. Then again, I've never personally witnessed this level of organizational maturity. Instead, the feature-based backlog always seems to dominate the other work, which inevitably undermines the overall quality of the team's efforts. In spite of this, I don't want to discourage anyone from trying this approach to see if it works within your context.

Future-Cast

This is related to the sheer size of your product backlog, but I want to pull it out separately. Beyond items, work tasks, etc., I think the product backlog provides a glimpse into the future that is extremely important to make transparent and actively share.

First of all, it helps stakeholders to understand the potential overall scope of the project effort. Traditional or Waterfall stakeholders often fall into a trap of wanting a broad universe early on in projects; way before the cost or feasibility of construction or value is clear. This _wish list view_ to requirements that are never renegotiated is extremely unrealistic and not useful. However, it does fit into Waterfall's upfront, contract-driven way of thinking.

The Agile / Scrum product backlog model is much healthier. It implies that stakeholders can put virtually anything on the list; as long as there is a clear priority. As the team makes incremental progress, it becomes increasingly clear to all participants, including stakeholders, as to what the team's capacity (velocity) is relative to the size of the backlog.

Additionally, as the team delivers incremental and high-value features, stakeholders realize incremental gains that change their views towards the remaining value of backlog items. Having a large backlog and understanding the team's capacity in working through it, velocity of Product Backlog Items or user stories achievable per sprint, can be a crucial step in managing these expectations towards more feasible goals.

Another part of Future-Casting is bundling sets of backlog features into customer release points. In my experience, release level planning is another of those weak points in many agile teams. They fall into a pattern of "sprint–at–time thinking" where everything of value is derived sprint-by-sprint. There is no cumulative construction of product features that are deployed as larger collections.

One by-product of this pattern is that the customer receives too frequent releases which dilutes the impact and increases their learning-to-value cost. It often fosters a scatter-shot approach within the agile team to deliver disparate features that don't integrate well to solve the customer's challenges.

Hopefully, this discussion has, at least, transformed your thinking regarding the product backlog being a _simple list_. While it is, it also isn't. It requires thought, strategy, care and feeding, expansion/contraction, and constant adjustment for you to effectively deliver value from your Scrum team.

Wrapping Up

❖ It's most important to keep the "tip" of your backlog iceberg ready for execution. You do this by vetting – discussing, estimating, and refining the stories, as well as including acceptance test definition, and improving the workflow of your team. This needs to be an iterative process or workflow that you schedule continuously with your teams during each sprint.

❖ Effective backlog management is about balance. Balance numbers, clarity / granularity, investment and value, and packaging. Each product / project team needs to achieve its own level given its unique technical and business context.

❖ Remember the 20/30/50 rule and maintain appropriate "tension" in your backlog. Don't be afraid to have a large list. It truly helps with scope understanding and negotiation. Just don't over-invest in the less important PBI's.

Chapter 7

'Grooming' the Product Backlog

While it may not be the best term, 'grooming' does help make the point that a Product Backlog is not a static thing. Instead, it's quite _organic_ in nature. It _should_ grow and it _should_ contract. Not everything on it should receive the same investment of time. Things at the _top_ should be quite granular and those at the _bottom_, merely a twinkle in someone's eye…usually coarsely grained and quite a large twinkle.

As you get work completed and items move up the backlog, they need to be further examined and refined. Those refinements could include:

- Having the team reconsider them based on their priority movement.
- Shuffle items around as you bundle stories into themes and consider effective sprint packing.
- Changing or reframing items as their original context may no longer be relevant.
- Breaking them down further, splitting them up, and refining their estimates.
- Having the team think about the prerequisites for each, the dependencies, and how best to package them into themes.
- Simply generating more conversations and thinking around work that is getting closer and closer to execution.

Grooming[26] the product backlog is a term I've heard used to refer to this iterative and continuous process. I've also heard the term Backlog Maintenance used. As with any organism, you need to be caring and feeding your backlog. This is at the team level, meaning the entire team working off of a particular backlog, should participate in its grooming. In this chapter we'll examine a few critical dynamics for keeping the beast well groomed, presentable and, more importantly, effective in driving each team's results.

---

[26] I've heard that in the UK, the term 'grooming' has a quite negative connotation. So backlog maintenance is a reasonable replacement if you don't want to use grooming. You might also consider Story Development. Whatever term you use, please do groom.

Scrum Guide Excerpt - Grooming

The Scrum Guide has the following excerpt which describes Schwaber and Sutherland's take on backlog grooming:

> Product Backlog grooming is the act of adding detail, estimates, and order to items in the Product Backlog. This is an ongoing process in which the Product Owner and the Development Team collaborate on the details of Product Backlog items. During Product Backlog grooming, items are reviewed and revised. However, they can be updated at any time by the Product Owner or at the Product Owner's discretion.

> Grooming is a part-time activity during a Sprint between the Product Owner and the Development Team. Often the Development Team has the domain knowledge to perform grooming itself. How and when grooming is done is decided by the Scrum Team. Grooming usually consumes no more than 10% of the capacity of the Development Team.

> The Development Team is responsible for all estimates. The Product Owner may influence the Development Team by helping understand and select trade-offs, but the people who will perform the work make the final estimate.

In the original *Scrum book* [27] I saw a reference to 10% time being reserved across the team for grooming. I've been making that recommendation to Scrum teams, with good results, for the past ten plus years. You see that recommendation above, but more so as a high-end limit. I actually think 10% is the right level of investment for teams; and remember, that's off the top of the teams' capacity in each and every sprint.

Grooming is Incredibly Nuanced

Many teams invest too little time in their backlog grooming. This might be justified if grooming was only a requirements practice, but it's not! It's an estimation and planning practice. It's an architectural and design practice.

---

[27] *Agile Software Development with Scrum*, published in 2001 by Ken Schwaber and Mike Beedle.

It's a dependency and risk planning practice. It's a quality and test planning practice. It's a technical research practice.

You have to realize that the backlog is the one artifact that encompasses all of the above in agile teams. You need to invest time and effort into grooming at all of these levels.

In my classes I even liken the backlog to the infamous *Work Breakdown Structure or WBS*[28] in project management. And I'm not joking with the students. In many ways the product backlog is THE planning artifact for your teams. And grooming is THE practice to ensure you have a thoughtful backlog (plan).

A Story – Your Sprint Planning Takes 'Forever'

As an agile coach, one of the Top 10 questions I get asked surrounds sprint planning. Things like: what are the typical meeting dynamics, should you introduce new work, what to do if the Product Owner isn't prepared, and how to handle a meeting that won't end are common questions. I guess it turns out that there are a lot of "ugly" planning meeting "out there" in the real world.

The latter question is an interesting one. I've come to the conclusion that there is a direct correlation between the quality (ease) of your sprint planning meeting and the investment & quality of your grooming.

If you regularly and actively groom your backlogs, then I think you're sprint planning meetings go much smoother. The team is prepared. The time is reduced. And the quality of the sprint plan, the execution and ultimately the results, are greatly enhanced.

If however, you've been short-sighted in your grooming, for example: if your next sprints' stories are ill-conceived and prepared, if your team is seeing the work for the very first time, or, if you skipped grooming entirely; then you are in for a wicked time.

---

[28] Work Breakdown Structure. I'm not going to define it, but I reference WBS as indicative of traditional project plans. Setting up tasks and workflows, analyzing estimates and trying to optimize the dependencies. At its core, the WBS is a hierarchical representation of a projects' work. More on it here: http://en.wikipedia.org/wiki/Work_breakdown_structure

So, the next time you have a sprint planning meeting that just doesn't quit, try to groom better before the next one. You just might be surprised with the results...

3 Common Metaphors for the Backlog

There are three metaphors that are commonly used to illustrate the dynamics of the backlog. They are:

1. **An Iceberg**: 90% of the stories should be course-grained, and "below the surface"; so we're not paying attention to them. I also like the principles of iceberg naturally 'calving' or breaking apart into smaller chunks.
2. **A Pyramid**: Again, the foundation is large and full of epics. The top or tip is what's interested. It does align with stones, which are a common metaphor for stories (*Boulders, Rocks, and Pebbles*[29]) granularity.
3. **A Conveyor Belt**: This is my own concoction. It indicates the organic nature, in that you are never 'done' with grooming. I also

---

[29] I wrote a blog post that tries to help with story sizing by using this metaphor. You can read more about it here: http://www.batimes.com/robert-galen/product-backlogs-boulders-rocks-and-pebbles%E2%80%A6oh-my.html

like the analogy of stories moving from an epic state towards sprint level execution. Getting smaller and smaller along the belt.

I find all of these useful in describing the dynamics of the backlog as teams continue to groom or refine their backlogs.

Beyond Stories, Consider Themes

When you're grooming your backlog, for the most part you're dealing with individual user stories. However, depending on the size of your project and subsequently the size of your backlog, it can be easy to get lost in the details by the sheer number of stories.

An extension from the story writing workshop (*discussed in Chapter 8*), along with some prioritization techniques, is to deal with your backlog in themes. Consider them groupings of stories that relate to specific functional requirements, roles, or sets of stories that are best executed together. This becomes even more important if you define finely grained user stories, in that it simplifies important aspects of grooming, the time it takes for prioritization and overall release planning.

Themes have another benefit. They help to explain the overall workflow to business stakeholders and customers in terms that are more meaningful to them. You'll start discussing sprint reviews and release plans within the context of your packaged themes.

Figure 4, provides an example of the typical workflow that is generated thematically for an agile project. It gives you a flavor for the workflow, and how themes need to be refocused and adjusted, as you approach each release point.

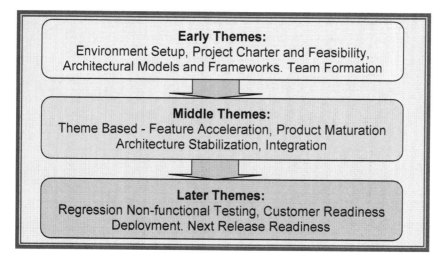

Figure 4, Typical workflow of themes leading to some sort of release point

Backlog Themes versus Time

Another characteristic of the backlog, in my way of thinking, is the relationship of ordering to time. For example, if you read it from top to bottom, higher priority to lower priority or now to later you'll gain an understanding of the strategy that you and your team are suggesting for implementing the next release or overall project.

Now, of course, things become fuzzy the further out in time we go. Even in these cases, if you're planning a product release in 3-4 sprints, then the backlog themes should change as you approach release. For example, there might be stories representing regression testing, or integration, or operational readiness training, or documentation and general sales training.

Now, let me caution you. This would be the flow when you're working in a context that doesn't *release to production* [30] at the end of every sprint. If your model is doing this, then you'll see these mini-strategies within each sprint's set of stories. As you extend the sprints that are building product or project value between actual releases, these strategies become more clearly visible throughout the backlog. It really depends on how you and your team have decided to deliver value towards your customers.

---

[30] A better way to articulate this is with the Agile Release Train metaphor. You can read much more about it in Chapter 16.
.

Grooming Dynamics

The ongoing discussions should continuously be focused towards qualifying your story INVEST (*discussed in Chapter 9*) characteristics; mostly by ensuring that they're of correct size, clarifying (or creating) the story and acceptance tests, and providing an initial estimate.

Inevitably, at least in all of my experiences, the team will digress into design discussions as they ask questions surrounding each story. This is quite helpful, as they're starting to align their thinking towards execution. You should foster this more and more as each story approaches sprint execution. But, only to such a degree that the team isn't being wasteful and/or getting hung up on too much detail…too soon.

Something I always remind teams of when they're grooming is the *Just-in-Time and Emergent* properties of agility. In the case of user stories, we want to defer some of the understanding till the point of picking up the card and implementing it. That's when we need and will gain the final details. More importantly, the team is gaining more information about each story as they get exposed to it again and again during each grooming session.

70% versus 30% Heuristic

I have a heuristic that I use with many teams to solidify this point. I use 70% and 30% as the targets. I recommend that a story is only defined to 70% clarity or completeness prior to entering a sprint. It should have open questions, holes, ambiguity, and unknowns; just not too many of them and not on in critical areas.

Why? Remember the stories are "intentionally incomplete" and that "they are a promise for a discussion". If we define them to 100% clarity, they won't drive any of that wonderful behavior.

So when does the remaining 30% get cleared up; why, when the story is executed within the sprint. The teams now fill in all of the gaps during the course of doing the work. This is one of the primary reasons that Product Owners need to be available to their teams; so that they can help fill in the blanks as the story unfolds.

Idea Generation

I've seen some great Product Owners vary the tempo of their grooming meetings or discussions so that there isn't the same focus all the time; that usually being, "Ask questions and then estimate this Story…"

They'll mix it up a bit. The first 15 minutes might be focused on introducing a few new stories or, perhaps, eliciting new ideas for stories from the team. This time is simply to chat about their viability and get an extremely high level estimate to help with initial prioritization and placement. Here they're also looking to generate brainstormed ideas for new ways to evolve the backlog towards the overall project and/or product goals.

Next, they'll switch gears and talk about the stories for the upcoming sprint. Gathering the most important ones into a theme and then talking about the business drivers for it. They might open the floor to discuss relationships and dependencies for stories within the theme. Is it the right set from a technical perspective? Can the entire theme be accomplished within the sprint? Do we need further adjustments to the stories? Breaking them up according to feasibility versus size versus overall theme needs becomes a point for discussion. Does the theme align with a coherent sprint goal? And does it lead to a compelling demonstration in the sprint review?

The meeting might then end with some requests for individuals to add acceptance tests for upcoming stories and/or requests for additional technical stories: bugs, refactoring opportunities, or research spikes. I like this part, because it pulls the entire team into the backlog as contributors.

This sort of round-robin approach to grooming the backlog keeps the team engaged and active, as well as, keeping the backlog fresh. It also sensitizes the team to the fact that grooming is a collaborative, iterative process that needs constant attention.

Group Grooming and Estimation Activity

There are two primary ways to perform backlog grooming, but they're not mutually exclusive. Most teams set aside some time each sprint for team-based grooming meetings. Others assign stories to team members for individual grooming before team-based discussion. Usually, the work is specific to a story, or a set of stories, that map to something in that person's background which make them a good candidate for the work.

Individual Backlog Maintenance

This approach has the advantage of being less disruptive to the team at-large and reasonably aligns grooming with the natural sprint-to-sprint workflow of the team. One of the disadvantages to this approach, and it's a large one, is that it isn't collaborative; so everyone is off, more or less, working and refining individual stories by themselves.

If you take this approach, you'll need a re-synch point before each sprint where the team is exposed to story conversations and feedback that has been going on individually. I've seen this take the form of a pre-sprint planning and estimating meeting where the team is exposed to a set of stories that are to be implemented in the next sprint. It's similar to sprint planning, but since the at-large team hasn't had exposure to the upcoming story set, it gives everyone the opportunity to gain familiarity.

Instead of the Product Owner being the only voice explaining each story, the team members who vetted them are also quite active in these sessions; explaining their thinking on how they composed and broke them down, how they came to their estimates, their thinking surrounding design, and around acceptance tests. The next approach is a variant of this meeting.

Group Backlog Maintenance

Instead of asking individuals to groom the backlog, this next approach is more collaborative and, thus, my favorite approach; although it does take a time investment across the team. Here, the Product Owner and Scrum Master schedule regular, periodic meetings during the course of each sprint. I've seen them oscillate between one and two times a week, for about an hour, in most teams.

These are grooming and estimation meetings. The product backlog is the central focus for the meeting where the Product Owner usually projects it on a screen and traverses it dynamically throughout the meeting. I described my preferred format earlier in this chapter under "Idea Generation" in which I explain that the Product Owner has several goals for the meeting agenda and keeps it lively by changing focus.

My experience shows that bi-weekly meetings are necessary when you're working on a *new or actively evolving backlog*[31]. For a mature backlog, less

---

[31] You might even need more meetings in the very beginning of new projects with new teams. Remember the 10% investment from the Scrum Guide. The point is –

frequent meetings are often the norm. Always keep in mind that you should try and re-visit each Story multiple times before execution.

A Combination

The reality is that I've used a combination of these two approaches to achieve the best results. Using collaborative meetings primarily, but also asking individuals to vet stories in advance. Usually these are the more complex or challenging stories. Ones where we need specific product or domain experience to fully flush out options for the team to consider; thus saving overall elaboration and discussion time.

As a recommendation, I think there are usually *about 20% of your backlog items*[32] that need some sort of individual attention, outside of the Product Owner, before vetting them with the larger team. These usually align with either technical or domain complexity.

Backlog Vetting Alternative: Technical Planning Meeting

At times, the team may need additional time to familiarize themselves with a set of features to be implemented in the next sprint. This is beyond the venue of their normal backlog grooming and estimation meetings. I've found this is usually needed in teams where you have complex or specialized domain-centric work coming up that the team, as a whole, isn't comfortable with. Often this happens in larger-scale projects or when there are many new team members.

The session allows the entire team to spend time on "pre-preparation" for the sprint fostering higher level design discussions, Q&A, and simple game planning for the upcoming work. More than likely, the Scrum Master and Product Owner won't attend. They'll simply kick-off the meeting and then leave. It's really the team's meeting; so, consider it a sort of group based design or code review, but at the sprint-based story level.

Normally, I'll time-box the meeting to 1-2 hours and schedule it a day or two before the sprint planning session. While I acknowledge that it's a little wasteful from a lean perspective, it can be a very powerful event by

---

you need to invest whatever time is required in backlog grooming to get it into a state to drive your execution. It takes what it takes; and it's that important!

[32] Just leveraging the Pareto Principle (again) here for guidance; or the 80/20 rule.

allowing the team to sort through global dependencies and technical details for a sprint's worth of work at the same time as brainstorming the best plan-of-attack.

In some contexts, I've come to the conclusion that this is a wonderful pre-cursor to normal sprint planning. One side-effect is that it puts the initiative clearly on the team's shoulders to prepare for the next sprint while giving them scheduled time to focus and work on it. If you've been lax in grooming the backlog in any way, this almost becomes a mandatory planning extension for your team.

A Grooming Story – Technical Complexity

I was once the Scrum Master for a team that was entering a sprint with a very complex body of work. All of the stories related to refactoring UI components of an existing legacy application and not all of the team members had familiarity with the legacy codebase. In fact, the team had two members who had only been onboard for 2-3 weeks.

While we had effectively groomed the backlog, I knew in my 'gut' that we weren't technically ready for the sprint planning meeting. We simply had not done enough "technical spike work" to understand what was about to be executed.

While I was worried about having an 'ugly' planning meeting, ultimately the concern was driven by sprint results. I felt quite sure we would ultimately fail to deliver anything meaningful in the next sprint. Then I had an idea.

I asked the team, not the Product Owner or myself, to have a technical grooming meeting. This was on Thursday, two days before sprint planning. I asked them to review code, review the stories, do a bit of early design, task some work out in advance, virtually anything they felt necessary to pre-stage their technical understanding of the upcoming work.

It took about two hours, but it worked beautifully. The team spent most of the time in the innards of the legacy code trying to figure out the high-level, technical game plan for the sprint. To a person, they felt the time and focus made all the difference in the sprint planning, but more importantly, in their confidence and the sprints ultimate execution and results.

Seeding the Backlog

One practice that I've seen work quite well is for the Product Owner to seed their backlogs with data in order to drive improved collaboration and feedback. That is, when you're creating a new backlog, or trying to foster further refinement, use your own ideas for story descriptions, acceptance tests, and *even estimates* [33]whenever possible. At times, try and say something that's either wrong or outrageous just to get the team's attention to drive discussion and refinements. It also encourages the team to *actively read* [34]and engage with the backlog.

My point here is that you don't need to bring every idea to your team "fully baked". Rather, bring your ideas and use that as a starting point. I've found that this creates a much richer discussion than simply providing an empty or minimal list. At the same time, share your strategy with your team so they understand what you're doing and why.

Grooming also Drives Communication

A colleague of mine, Tony Brill, likes to remind me that one of the key roles of a great Product Owner is driving communication across a broad range of interested parties. As is usually the case, he's right. The backlog needs to become a central point, not only for the work, but for discussing all aspects of what needs to be done. It should draw customers, management, team members, other teams, and stakeholders into crisp discussion surrounding how to best accomplish your goals.

Given this, not all forms of backlog items are conducive or effective in driving all kinds of communication. Sometimes you want to be involved with finely grained story details, and at other times, it's more effective to deal with epics. Tony has come up with a Product Owner communication matrix that maps to backlog items in Figure 5.

---

[33] Often some team members won't engage with the backlog the way you hope. Seeding has a way of drawing them back into the backlog; particularly when you start making estimates "for them".

[34] In a "perfect world", I like to see each team member viewing/interacting with their Product Backlog on a daily basis. Have it up on their monitor: reviewing stories, improving their content, asking questions, splitting them up, and providing early estimates are all "fair game". It says to me that the team is operating as a 'Village' on their backlog.

The bold items indicate the preferred backlog item level for communication given the role and style of communication you're exploring. The important point here is to effectively adjust the granularity of your discussion as your audience varies.

Role	Exploring Opportunities	Suggesting Solutions	Facilitating Collaboration	Understanding the Marketplace
Customers	Epic / Theme	Epic / Theme		Epic / Theme
Management	Epic	Theme	Theme	Epic / Theme
Your team	Theme / Story	Theme / Story		Theme
Other teams	Story	Story	Story	Theme
Stakeholders	Theme	Story	Story	Theme

Figure 5, Product Owner – Backlog Communication Levels

Wrapping Up

❖ Groom your backlog consistently at different levels: new stories, revisited stories, looking for themes, right before sprint planning, etc. Remember it's a dynamic list. I prefer a general rule that I revisit each user story on the backlog at least 3 times prior to its implementation.

❖ Actively engage your team in the grooming process. Measure your success by the number of initiative based backlog changes that the team introduces, as each team member should be adding, changing, decomposing, and removing backlog items.

❖ Individual research is an important part of backlog maturation. Engage specific Subject Matter Experts and other team members by using judicious research spikes to flush out the challenging bits. Also, there's no rule against team members doing a bit of "personal research" in addition to spikes on the backlog.

Chapter 8

Creating the Product Backlog

A great Product Owner does not go it alone when they're creating the initial Product Backlog. In fact, they should engage their entire team in the process. Often _starting_ to create the backlog can be quite intimidating. You simply don't know how, or where, to start. There's a technique that Mike Cohn introduces in his User Stories book that maps to running a _User Story Writing Workshop_ as a means of establishing an initial product backlog.

The idea has, at its roots, the same dynamics as JAD (Joint Application Development) workshops or similar requirements and planning techniques. These team-based collaborative approaches have been used effectively since well before the rise of the agile methodologies. Essentially, you invite your potential or current team in a room along with the set of _engaged stakeholders_ for your project effort. Get as many individuals, as you can, who will have a vested interest in the project or product outcomes.

Another important aspect is cross-functional attendance. For example, you'll want developers, testers, technical writers, trainers, support personnel, perhaps a sales person or two, and other Product Owners. You're trying to gain as broad a spectrum of functional coverage as possible to represent the various organizational stakeholders for your project.

Even the developers can be difficult to broadly engage because of their various functional areas. You'll want attendance from business analysts and architects. If you have multiple tiers to your product development, then each tier needs representation, for example web UI, middleware, and back-end databases.

A Story – Don't Go It Alone

I met a Product Owner not that long ago who was quite stressed out. He was relatively new to his company. While he had some agile experience, being immersed into a new agile environment, team and domain was quite intimidating.

I came into the organization as a coach and was just trying to get a sense for the environment. He quickly pulled me aside and confronted me with a problem. He complained that he simply didn't have the time to construct stories, or a backlog for his team.

It turned out that he'd been working into the night for the past 2 weeks to get an initial backlog together. His team was "waiting for it" and it was taking him a long time to get the backlog completed. He was struggling with his domain experience and technical understanding of the products underlying architecture. He was also struggling with writing effective acceptance tests for the stories. Since he was new, he kept working on them; trying to create the "perfect backlog" before 'presenting' it to his team.

I can't tell you how stressed out and exhausted he was.

I suspect my reaction might have seemed odd to him. I asked him to immediately stop working on the backlog stories. Instead, I asked him to schedule a story-writing workshop where he, and his team, would sit down and create the backlog TOGETHER. I told him to bring his current story mix into the meeting - as-is. It would serve as a nice starting point for the team.

I reminded him that the Product Owner shouldn't 'own' writing all the stories; that the Product Owner role was more of a backlog facilitative role. I also reminded him to leverage the whole team in crafting a solid backlog and that he never had to "go it alone" in preparing a backlog.

I ran into him after the first workshop and he appeared incredibly relieved. He said the workshop was outstanding and he was amazed at the ability of his new team to rally around fleshing out his ideas. His renewed energy and enthusiasm were music to my ears.

Setting the Stage

Probably the most important step in driving a successful story-writing workshop is preparation. While that's true of any collaborative meeting, where you want participants to produce artifacts, it's particularly important here.

Also, keep in mind that this is *your* meeting. You should be center stage; clearly providing the vision and setting clear goals, listening intently to your team, always getting them to focus on goals, while detecting adjustments that need to be made. Answering any and all questions; taking actions when you need more research, then ensuring effective follow-up. Remember, you're not simply using the teams and other stakeholders' time to create stories for your backlog. Instead, this is your first step at *crafting a clear and powerful product or project direction for your team*.

Here are a few preparation steps that I recommend you consider when planning your own workshops:

1. **Provide Product Vision**: The essence of a story writing workshop is to produce a broad and deep set of user stories (requirements, tasks, steps, and actions) that will encompass the product or project work to be completed; essentially, the product backlog. In order to get the desired breadth, you'll need to bring enough *character* to the meeting regarding the nature of the effort. I often find it useful to include others in communicating these points, such as key stakeholders and/or leaders from the business-side or architects from the technology-side.

2. **Define Key Goals:** Think of these as the compelling value propositions for the project. They should include not only key areas of customer value, 1-2-3 central focus points; but, also key dates or schedule targets, high value feature sets, quality targets, competitive pressure points, etc.

   Think of these first two points as relating to your Project Charter, which we explore in more detail in Chapter 12.

3. **Establish Meeting Structure and Organization:** As I mentioned earlier, care must be taken to get the *right* set of constituents together to maximize your results. This is a breadth versus depth balancing act, but remember, this is your first stab at the product

backlog, so you don't need to include _everyone,_ as there will be plenty of opportunity for future collaboration.

I like to organize the meeting into several phases as illustrated here:

o **Phase 1:** Introduce the project vision and primary goal(s). Also, cover primary requirements / feature sets of the product or project at a very high level. Explaining key usage scenarios or workflows can be quite helpful here.

o **Phase 2:** Brainstorm the relevant user roles that will help focus the story writing in the workshop. This includes more natural user roles, as well as, system or external interface point roles. If you have a regulated environment, now would be a good time to assign these support responsibilities to a role.

o **Phase 3:** Of course the majority of the meeting is focused towards user story brainstorming and development. In this case, for each role, dig down and brainstorm a set of stories. Round-robin through all of the roles. Categorization, organization, and grouping into themes can be a natural outcome of this phase. I usually time-box the individual role brainstorming to about 5-10 minutes per role, including story clarification.

o **Phase 4**: Spend some time prioritizing an initial set of themes and stories for execution. You don't have to order the entire list at this point, but look for clear winners when it comes to business value and establishing early technical value.

Establish your own agenda around these or other phases and allow for sufficient time for collaboration and discussion.

Depending on the size of your project and team, the entire meeting should be time-boxed from about 2 to 8 hours. I usually time-box each of the phases and prefer to be aggressive with the times; finding it easier to schedule another meeting rather than going on too long and exhausting the team's enthusiasm.

4. **Define Your Role:** Gather your thoughts around your own product ownership role within the meeting. Clearly, you need to be the one setting the stage for the outcome, especially since it's _your_ product or project. But, what part will you play in fostering thinking around good stories? Or, answering questions? Or, capturing information? I've often found it useful for the Product Owner to occasionally _seed_ the meeting with a set of roles and high-level stories that will serve to focus the meeting in broader terms. This usually gives the team something to feed off of and, normally, results in a better mix of stories.

5. **Effective Facilitation:** The success of the meeting depends, as much on the facilitator, as any other preparation aspect. Facilitation is an art and not everyone can perform it well. It requires some experience within the product and project organization and, at least, a superficial understanding of the problem space.

   However, the real key is finding someone who has facilitated collaborative meetings before, has _a toolbox of facilitative techniques_ [35](yes, such things do exist), and an understanding of how to crisply move the team forward without losing valuable collaboration and ideas.

   Another suggestion is to find someone that can _scribe_ the results of the meeting on-the-fly. This will help immensely in generating post-meeting momentum.

Importance of Roles

As you approach a story-writing workshop, you have a decision to make. Do you dive in and simply start writing stories or do you try and provide some direction and structure to your story development via roles. I've found it incredibly useful to first brainstorm the key system roles and then develop your stories within or under each role.

Think of roles in the sense of lightweight _Personas_ for actual users of the system you're about to develop or, if you're familiar with use cases, as the

---

[35] Jean Tabaka's _Collaboration Explained_ book (see references) is quite helpful here. As-is another book: _Great Meetings! – Great Results_ by Dee Kelsey and Pam Plumb is one of the best facilitative tools books that I've found.

primary Actors [36]within your system. The roles will cover physical users, for example: novice user, expert user, administrative user, non-English speaking user, etc., as well as, system-focused roles, for example: B2B systems, the diagnostic sub-system, the auto-update system, etc. All relevant systems, components, or interface points should be included.

I've found that starting with a broad set of roles, then consolidating and organizing them into a subset of meaningful groups, improves the overall quality of your user story writing by increasing the depth and breadth.

It also serves as a focusing mechanism. Instead of everyone writing stories from the perspective of the generic user, it gives everyone a much narrower focus on a per-role basis to engage their thinking. The key point here is: always try to start your story-writing workshop with role definition. It will make a huge _difference_[37]!

Basic Deliverable or Outcomes

However you approach it, in the end I like to exit a story-writing workshop with the following outcomes and deliverables:

- An estimated 80% mix of relevant stories for the project or product being surfaced and captured. Most are ill defined and epic-sized, but a solid starting point.

- A very, very rough backlog in sequencing or ordering. I think of the ordering in terms of thirds, with the top, middle, and bottom third of all the items are appropriately fitted in time.

- The top third should include the _Must Have's_. It's never too early to start sensitizing your stakeholders and team on what's truly important. There should also be some theme-based groupings in this

---

[36] I believe there is synergy between agile use cases and user stories. One of the key areas is in the definition of roles vs. actors. I'd argue they are the same. In fact, the use case view of secondary vs. primary actors might be useful within a story context.

[37] Roles can also help align with Themes and Groupings when it comes to prioritizing your User Stories. For example, if you have a Legislative User role that is more important than other roles, then organizing along this boundary helps focus on that distinction.

section.

- Of crucial importance is coming out with follow-up actions; either planning for follow-up estimation, as well as, drafting release and/or sprint plans.

- If anyone had an initial, high-level estimate for a story, then certainly capture it. Otherwise, there are no estimates. These would begin to surface in the first product backlog grooming and estimation meetings, which we'll explore later in Chapter 10.

Figure 6, gives you a visualization of what your backlog should look like exiting your workshop: lots of stories, simple theme-based groupings, and execution time-based prioritization.

Warning: You May Get Lots of "Stuff"

It's quite common to exit the workshop with a very large and intimidating backlog. Remember, you'll want to surface all of the work to make the overall scope visible. However, product or project release planning will partition your backlog into feature sets, customer release points, and manageable chunks of high-value functionality.

You will probably never get to all the work. That's more or less by design; driven by the lean strategies within the methods. So, don't become concerned over an initially large backlog. Stay more focused towards the top of it along with your first and second release points. Progress, time, value, and stakeholder feedback will always clarify the remainder!

Story Brainstorming Workshop Story

Our CEO at ChannelAdvisor had a brilliant idea once for a new addition to our eCommerce application suite. We were a mature, SaaS (Software as a Servic) startup and were working incredibly hard to compete in a harsh competitive landscape. So he asked us to vet his idea. On the surface, he felt that it would only take a few engineers, a few weeks to implement. To be fair, every idea he had was roughly this same approximate size ;-)

He wanted us to dive-in and start implementation immediately. While we 'heard' him, we were a fairly mature Scrum shop and we decided to run a story brainstorming workshop to ascertain the true level of effort behind the idea.

We invited a cross-functional team together. In about 2-3 hours, we brainstormed a series of epics/stories that represented, at a high-level, all of the work we could envision to properly implement his request. We had about 220 story cards on a wall. During that time, we also did a high level sizing of the stories and laid them out in priority or execution ordering. Just to get a sense of how may sprints and teams it would take to implement the new component.

It turned out that it would have taken ¾ of our overall engineering team (about 6 teams) about a full release cycle, (4, 2-week sprints), to deliver this component. So it would have disrupted about 6 months of our existing roadmap & release plans.

When we told our CEO that it would take about 10-15x what he thought it would take in effort, he passed on the feature as not being cost justified and a poor business decision. The "good news" was that it took us only 3+ hours to figure that out AND we didn't start the work first...

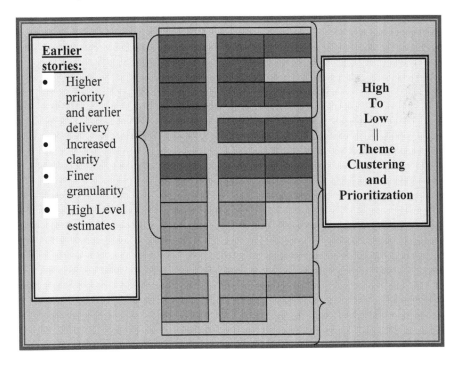

Figure 6, Visual story outcome of Story Writing Workshop

Stories Are a Practiced Skill

Even though user stories are a highly accepted means for capturing agile requirements, there is still much confusion in the community surrounding their development. The confusion is exacerbated by two factors. First, there are not many solid, real word examples in the agile community; either on the internet or in books.

As I said, Mike Cohn has written the definitive text on the subject but, this too, is void of detailed examples of user story specifics and hierarchy for a complex project. The other factor is driven by the very nature of agility. It is not an artifact-driven methodology; instead, it is a conversation and collaboration-driven methodology. So, user stories are intentionally brief and ambiguous.

The good news here, from a story writing perspective, is simply to _Dive In_ and start writing stories for your application and business domain. Just do it! Don't get hung up on one versus two-sentence structure, or completeness, or every story needing the same length or phrasing. Instead, just do your best, use common sense, trust your team, and just do it.

Over time, as everyone gains experience, you and your team will improve in their story writing skills. Your skill will naturally relate to your project, domain, and team because the story structure and needs adapt to each team's specific context. Also, remember that with each sprint, there is a sprint retrospective. Early on, you should naturally discuss user story writing, estimation, and planning improvements in your retrospectives as part of your natural inspect and adapt practices.

Wrapping Up

❖ User Stories, while not a panacea, are a wonderful way to capture requirements in your product backlog. Try using them. If you don't like user stories, you always can use traditional requirement specifications or 'Agile' use cases. Remember, the backlog is simply a list of things to do, so don't get too hung up on format.

❖ Collaborate with your team and stakeholders when mining for requirements, ordering them, and planning their workflow. Do this often as part of your general transparency, not only into the what, but also for the how and how long of your stories.

❖ Leverage roles as a means of driving a richer set of stories. Remember that there are pure user-oriented roles and other, non-user roles such as API's, security risks, regulatory agencies, third party / contractual users, test applications, etc. Create a broad and rich set of roles, but don't create too many - 3 to 8 is probably a good mix to start with.

❖ Practice writing your stories! Effective story writing is a practiced skill and somewhat unique to the demands of each specific Scrum team. Be patient and work hard (as a team!) to gain experience in writing stories that _guide_ your application development efforts.

Chapter 9

Writing User Stories

Great Product Owners should have some skill surrounding user story writing. They need to particularly know what makes a good story, when is it too short, too long, or just right. They also have to buy into the *philosophy* behind the user story artifact, where team collaboration and conversation is the most important element.

That it's designed to be intentionally incomplete, which fosters much in the way of discussion and debate amongst the team members tasked with implementing it. Most importantly, the very use will place *positive pressure* on the Product Owner to engage with the team in discussing details towards implementing specifically what you have asked for.

Three C's

As a starting point, it's useful to consider the 3 C's behind the user story. The notion was first defined by *Ron Jeffries* [38]as a heuristic to guide story writing. The 3 C's are:

1. **Card:** Represents the story card itself, either a 3x5 index card or Post-it Note that represents the user story. Written on the card or note is the story; simply one or two sentences that captures a simple and clear description of each requirement.

2. **Confirmation:** Represents the acceptance tests or criteria for the story. These compliment the story description and help to clarify what behavior the story needs to exhibit. It's the Card (Description), along with the Confirmation (Acceptance Tests), that provide the textual description for the feature or function being requested.

3. **Conversation:** Finally, and most importantly, there are the conversations that surround the story during its development. I usually envision a developer grabbing a story card from the planning wall. The first thing he/she does is review the context of

---

[38] Ron Jeffries defined it as part of his XP work in – www.xprogramming.com

the story within the technical landscape they are developing in; just for a few minutes - thinking of design and construction steps. The very next thing they would do is *gather* other developers, testers and the Product Owner to talk about the implementation from each of their unique perspectives.

They all craft a common view to the story and the part each will play in implementation. They then go about developing the feature, pairing together whenever it makes sense. The goal is to collaboratively deliver the story without later re-work; meaning it *meets* the Product Owner's vision, confirmed by the acceptance tests.

The most important C again, is conversation. To my thinking, the confirmation (acceptance tests) is next in importance and the card (description) itself is of least import.

What Ron is really trying to emphasize here is the third tenant of the Agile Manifesto—

"Customer Collaboration over Contract Negotiation"

In this case I'd extend that to include—

"Customer and Team Collaboration at All Costs"

The entire point to the user story is not to get it perfectly or precisely defined in advance. The story is really a *promise to have a conversation* surrounding the work at the point of attack. It's this deferred clarification that is so powerful. You actually write stories with intentional ambiguity, knowing that you'll resolve much of it during your team's sprint collaborative conversations.

As a Product Owner, this is the reason your agile team needs you to be *available*. Not to ruin your day or waste your time, but to include *face-to-face communication*[39] as your primary means of sharing customer needs and context.

---

[39] Why face-to-face communication? Studies have shown that our communication falls into 3 categories—words, tone, and body language. Across these, information is transferred at a 15%, 35% and 50% rates respectively. Clearly written

A Story Framework

Figure 7, represents a model framework for crafting the format of a solid user story. It first focuses on the user role, or persona, that the story is targeting. The next focus is on the description of functionality. The final point is the value proposition or what problem are we trying to solve.

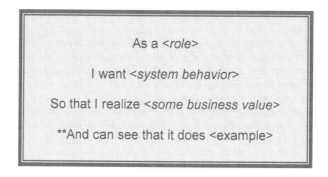

As a *<role>*

I want *<system behavior>*

So that I realize *<some business value>*

**And can see that it does <example>

Figure 7, Story Writing Framework

A recent addition to the framework adds an example to the user story. I think of this as mostly a usage scenario that can be executed to confirm the story meets your overall acceptance; so it's a bit of an extension to the confirmation part, but it would be the most important confirmation.

Then on the back of the card are detailed acceptance tests, which are the formal confirmation part of the story. These are not intended to be exhaustive functional tests in the traditional software testing or Quality Assurance sense. Instead, they focus on the business logic tests that identify crucial aspects of the story. Typically, there may be between 5 to 10 acceptance tests in the form of "Verify that…" or "Confirm that…" on the back of the card.

As an example, the following story in Figure 8 for a pet-sitting service, details a set of acceptance tests that provide additional functional descriptiveness for the developers and testers to more fully understand, and therefore implement the story.

---

documentation, while comfortable for many of us introverts, is the lowest bandwidth method, and while face-to-face is the richest and achieves 100% information transfer.

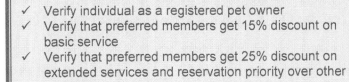

> As a dog owner, I want to sign-up for a kennel reservation over Christmas so that I can get a confirmed spot.

> ✓ Verify individual as a registered pet owner
> ✓ Verify that preferred members get 15% discount on basic service
> ✓ Verify that preferred members get 25% discount on extended services and reservation priority over other members
> ✓ Verify that past Christmas customers get reservation priority
> ✓ Verify that declines get an email with a discount coupon for future services

Figure 8, Story writing framework with examples of acceptance tests

A Story – Don't let format get in the way!

While I'm typically a stickler for writing stories properly, I've seen many teams let the writing of stories become an exercise in perfection. They relentlessly pursue writing the perfect story on the very first try.

They'll debate the wording of the acceptance tests and take literally an hour to write a few. Or debate whether they need to add another story versus an acceptance test. They also will argue incessantly whether a story is 2 versus 3 versus 5 points in size.

There can be an awful lot of debate around user roles as well. While proper story writing is important AND the discussions are valuable, these teams are missing one of the most important parts of user story writing:

It's iterative!

I usually coach them to get something…anything…on a card as a starting point. I actually don't even care if the initial story adheres to the framework or not. Just "put some words down" as a starting point and we can iterate from there.

Don't let the pursuit of story perfection infect your teams...

Don't Go It Alone

Many Product Owners attack user story development from the perspective that it's solely their responsibility to develop them. However, nothing could be further from the truth. Instead view the development of your backlogs as a team responsibility that only starts with the story-writing workshop; it does not end there.

Virtually anyone on the team can and should add or, much more importantly, refine stories within the backlog. This applies to the story description and the acceptance tests. If you have traditional business analyst roles within your team, then they can certainly take on much of this work. If you don't, then your testers can adopt much of it. In fact, the development of a set of good acceptance tests falls nicely into the realm of the testers on your team and they can help immensely here.

Story Characteristics

As you develop your stories, there's another heuristic to keep in mind that will help you develop a set of solid and properly framed user stories. It's the INVEST acronym and it guides you towards stories that are:

1. **Independent:** As much as is possible, user stories need to be developed so that they are independent of other stories. This becomes important during prioritization for execution. If every story depends on another, then your sprint planning becomes nearly impossible to orchestrate.

2. **Negotiable:** You want them to be clear enough, from a business and value perspective, so that you, the team, and stakeholders can individually negotiate each story.

3. **Valuable:** Related to negotiability, each story should be prioritized in the order that it brings value (priority) to the business and customer. Each priority should be unique as well, so for example, a list of system backup features can't all be first priority.

4. **Estimate-able:** One of the more important aspects of backlog stories is that their size is estimated so that the Product Owner understands the <u>level of complexity</u> and <u>level of effort</u> associated with each. The point here is that they should be relatively self-contained, with few dependencies, and small enough to be sized effectively.

5. **Small**: Related to estimate-able, your stories need to be correctly sized. First for proper estimation. But, not just for that. It also helps in, what I refer to as sprint packing to have smaller stories. Ones that can be completed by an individual or a small group within 2-3-4 days will assure that you can efficiently align work within your sprints.

6. **Testable:** Finally a focus on acceptance! Each story should be testable and acceptance tests need to clearly delineate those conditions. For example, a tax calculation feature and all variant interest rate calculation boundaries should be clearly defined as acceptance tests. In addition, all negative variants should also be defined.

When you're following INVEST in your story writing, don't get hung up on meeting each characteristic for every story. For example, you certainly will have dependent stories in most applications. The important point is to avoid, reduce, or contain them the majority of the time.

There are also some characteristics that, I believe, are non-negotiable, testable being one of those. As a rule, I expect ALL user stories to have an appropriate number and level of acceptance tests that are *derived with and approved by* [40]the Product Owner prior to that story making it into a sprint.

Story Execution Readiness

We will discuss user story prioritization in another chapter; however, I want to wrap-up this one up with the notion of readiness. Great Product Owners define done-ness at many levels when operating within their roles. The lowest level is at the individual user story. You need to ensure that your stories are well written: short, clear, properly ambiguous, and with a full set of acceptance tests.

---

[40] I know I'm being a stickler here, but it goes back to the Agile Manifesto point of valuing <u>Working Software</u> over writing about software.

Foster an environment within the team where everyone collaborates on refining the stories. Nonetheless, the buck should stop with you when stories approach a sprint for execution. They need to be excellent in their definition along with pre-vetting them by effective grooming within the team. There's no worse feeling than having an ill-conceived or defined user story hit the team in sprint planning that causes an hour or two of discussion and debate. I've been there and it's awful. Great Product Owners don't allow this to happen and it's here that we're going next.

Readiness Criteria

Just to help make this point, here's an example of user story readiness criteria:

- The story is well-written; and has a minimum of 5 acceptance tests defined.
- The story has been sized to fit the teams' velocity & sprint length: 1-13 points.
- The team has vetted the story in several grooming sessions—its scope & nature is well understood.
- If required, the story had a research-spike to explore (and refine) its architecture and design implications.
- The team understands how to approach the testing of the stories' functional and non-functional aspects.
- Any dependencies to other stories and/or teams have been "connected" so that the story is synchronized and deliverable.
- The story aligns with the sprints' goal and is demonstrable.

Unless every story passes this checklist, it should not be allowed to enter a teams' next sprint for execution.

Wrapping Up

❖ Communication can and will recover ill-defined stories, so all 3 C's are important, but communication rocks! I think of this in terms of when the story is ready for execution – the team responsible for coding, testing, documenting and delivering the story needs to "huddle up" and figure out how they'll be doing it. Asking the Product Owner questions and engaging them in the evolution of the story through to interim 'acceptance' within the context of the current sprint.

❖ The Product Owner doesn't have to write all of the user stories. In fact, I think in healthy teams they perform very little beyond _seeding_ the initial lists and capturing user story workshop results. Leverage business analysts and testers as _key partners_ in developing well-defined user stories. And the team as a whole plays a key role in it too…since it's really THEIR backlog!

Chapter 10

Managing the Initial Product Backlog

Great Product Owners don't simply stop working on the backlog after a story-writing workshop or after their first completed list. Indeed, their journey has just begun. In this chapter I want to share some tools for handling backlog item prioritization and estimation. You and your team will find them useful when you _groom_ your backlogs during your sprints.

Tools for Handling Priority

When I first read about Scrum and began applying it to my software projects, priority was something that appeared quite simple. The Product Owner was supposed to order the product backlog to reflect ongoing business priority (value) of the items on the backlog. Nothing could be simpler – right?

Then, as my experience grew, I realized that things were not quite that easy. There was a lot of nuance in priority because it reflected the _workflow_ for the project. That is, if _all_ work for a project effort is on the backlog and the order implies execution workflow over time, then the Product Owner cannot make priority decisions in a vacuum solely through a business-centric lens.

Priority has to be nuanced and considered against other factors, for example:

1. **Business value**: For user stories that represent features, then this is relatively clear. For tasks, research spikes, re-factoring work, training, bug fixes, etc. the distinction isn't quite so clear, but it's equally important. Therefore, business value needs to be _carefully weighed_[41] against a wide range of work.

2. **Time value**: If you view the backlog as a representation of a project schedule, then timing of delivery truly matters. For example, if you need to perform some work on testing infrastructure, then doing it too late in the release sequence simply devalues its impact

---

[41] This highlights one of the advantages to keeping business focused work versus other work in separate Backlogs as I discussed in Chapter 4—the partitioning can sometimes lead to clearer decision-making.

on the project; just as deferring any critical bug fixes until the final sprint is a poor strategy.

3. **Dependency value**: While we desire independence (the "I" in INVEST) as a prerequisite for good user stories, the harsh reality is that there will be strong dependencies that come into play for meaningful execution. These will need to be accommodated as you plan for delivery. A good example of this is a set or theme of stories that implement a specific customer workflow for a release. They will all need to be delivered together to realize the value.

   Another good example is to have multiple teams working on sets of stories that have cross-team dependencies, at the same time. Then the stories would need to be integrated to realize their full value or potential.

4. **Technical value**: If you're collaborating effectively with your team, you realize that their opinions on technical flow are important. So, when you implement features from a development perspective considering architecture or infrastructural dependencies, ease of implementation, natural flow of implementation, ease of testing, and team member availability; all of which fundamentally matters from an efficiency and cohesion perspective. It also helps team morale if you listen to, and consider, their expertise and overall availability.

For factors 2-4, great Product Owners truly engage in collaborative planning with their teams to surface, consider, and effectively prioritize in a truly nuanced fashion.

Said differently, it's never a good idea to prioritize simply based on Business Value.

Group Based Prioritization

If you're working on a larger-scale project of any complexity, please prioritize at the group or theme level as much as possible.

Of course, you first uniquely prioritize every element in your product backlog. However, once you start truly debating priorities and sweating the details, take a lesson from how most agile projects plan and set your priorities at a level above the individual user story. Work more at the level of groups of related stories, or themes of stories that combine to deliver necessary and related value to the customer.

Working at this level will accomplish two important things. First, it will keep you and your team out of the details or weeds. And this is a pattern I see in many agile teams. They dive into the details too soon. So the more you can work on 'collections' of items, the better.

The other thing it will help is in effectively identifying sprint goals, which also lead to more focused sprint reviews. Too many teams consider individual stories when executing a sprint. I'd much rather have them view the sprint from a cohesive goal perspective, which maps nicely to thematic composition of stories within your product backlogs.

Next we'll examine two of the *simpler tools* [42] that can be used for post story writing grouping and prioritization.

Affinity Grouping – Themes

Affinity grouping is a very simple technique that is again, collaborative. Working with the stakeholders and team, place all your user stories on the table. If you have a sufficient number of people, you can break into smaller sub-teams with subsets of stories.

Each group turns over a story card and briefly discusses what group or theme it might best be included with; creating group categories on-the-fly and freely moving stories around dynamically; either on a table or on a wall. The idea is to look for natural affinity across the team as stories _cluster_ where it makes the most sense to implement them.

As discussion and the grouping progresses, the team establishes a hierarchical set of groups that encompass the major components of the system or project being undertaken. This sets the stage for later prioritization at a group or theme level.

---

[42] I might sound like his spokesperson by now, but Mike Cohn has written the definitive book when it comes to agile prioritization techniques. I've chosen to illustrate some simple ones here. There are many more ideas in his _Agile Estimation and Planning_ book.

Priority Poker

Priority Poker is another fast technique that can be used to make a comparative distinction between stories. It's not that useful for identifying individual priorities for large sets of user stories, say for a 1000 of them. However, if you've packaged stories into themes, and have perhaps 10-50 to prioritize, then there is no faster way to develop a rough view to the ordering of those themes than by using priority poker.

Here's how it works.

Everyone gets a set of cards from 1...9, 1 representing the highest priority; 9, the lowest. A group of user stories or a theme is selected and each discussed in turn. Not too much discussion though! Afterward, the team will throw their cards down with their priority calls. Members with high and low values quickly explain their thinking so you can optionally discuss, re-vote, and debate until you converge on a value that the group determines is valid. Then you move onto the next. A word of advice here is to let the voting drive the discussion – so vote often.

There are several variations on this technique that can prove valuable. The first one is placing some sort of limits or boundaries on priority levels. For example, limiting the number of priority 1 thru 3 Stories to about 20-30% of your entire story portfolio or mix will make for some interesting discussions and/or debates. It also creates a more realistic and *varied curve* [43] in your story priorities, i.e., influencing a trend so that not every story will be number one in priority.

Another variation is adding the notion of value. Each estimator receives a "pool of funds" to spread across their backlog story prioritization decision-making. For example, you might get an overall pool of $50,000 to spend on your story 'votes'. A priority 1 might cost you $5,000, while a priority 5 might cost $500.

No bargaining is allowed and all/or nothing may be an option. As you're voting on priority, each number 1...9 has a specific cost that is paid after making that vote. Not only does this change your thinking and focus on

---

[43] I discussed the 20/30/50 Backlog focus relationship in Chapter , which supports this view.

value as it relates to priority, but it also forces you to make balanced decisions across your portfolio of themes and their priorities.

There are certainly other ways to attack this, so be creative within your team. Also be selective, focusing on the _now_ stories versus future stories that you might never get to.

High Level Estimates – Units?

There's a tremendous amount of discussion in the agile community around estimation of backlog items. If you're using user stories, then a common practice is to estimate them in story points.

If you're familiar with Function Points or Use Case Points, then Story Points are _not_ the same. In the former cases, you actually try to size your application in these units (points) so that they can be directly correlated to time, which leads to effort cost and schedule planning. With story points, you actually try and stay away from this time conversion thinking.

Instead story points are a unit-less measure that tries to capture _approximate and relative_ size and complexity for each user story. So, why is this useful you might ask?

Because when you're prioritizing your product backlog and ordering stories into themes, then relative size and complexity becomes a vital factor. In other words, 10 extremely complex stories are not equal to 10 very trivial stories. So, measuring 10 stories as a team capacity or velocity, needs some sort of relative size and complexity weighting to make the velocity indicator meaningful across a _varied set_ of stories.

It also helps you and your team to plan out how many stories can be done in a sprint by packaging up sets of stories into themes. As you execute these themes, you get a sense for not how many stories you can do, which varies considerably, by measuring your story point capacity per sprint. It turns out that this is a much steadier metric of your team's performance or output capacity (velocity) sprint over sprint.

Finally, after you've executed a few sprints, you can start measuring your team's velocity in story points, in other words – "We can deliver _about_ 25 story points in a 2-week sprint".

That knowledge can be extremely useful when doing release planning on your product backlog. Answering the inevitable question of: when will the _entire_ project be complete? Story point estimates give you a forecasting mechanism for determining your response to these and other questions while predicting more traditional project completion time-frames.

Again, I can't begin to do it justice in this short space, so reference Mike Cohn's book for a much more detailed explanation of the approach.

Two Level Agile Planning Abstraction

Remember, even though it might be tempting and relatively easy to convert your story points to represent time, try not to. It's important to keep in mind that it's a rough sizing, level of effort, complexity component, and not directly tied to time. If you do start tying it directly to time, your team will get anxious, start padding, fudging or manipulating their estimates. It's a more honest and valuable metric if you leave, or try as much as possible, to leave time out of it.

Remember, too, that Scrum and other agile methods maintain a _2 level planning abstraction_ that I will illustrate below:

- **High Level Planning is performed at the Product Backlog level when:**
    - Stories and story points are captured and estimated
    - Release plans are forecast at the velocity level for sets of or themes of Product Backlog Items or user stories
    - Stakeholder commitments are _lightweight and variable_—as progress is made and your understanding of level of effort improves

- **Low Level Planning is done at the Sprint – Sprint Backlog level when:**
    - This is where stories are broken down into tasks
    - Where the true effort for each sprint is surfaced
    - Where true time emerges
    - Connects to your high level plans—as the team works together, as they come to understand more, as their skill on this project increases…ALL estimates become more accurate (triangulate) over time

This implies that all product backlog / Product Owner driven planning is best kept at the higher level. While it is less detailed and ambiguous, it does abstract you and the team from diving to deeply into the details too quickly.

Planning Poker

There's a high level estimation technique that is quite popular in the agile and Scrum community called *Planning Poker[44]*. It is a derivative of the *Wideband Delphi* [45] technique where you gather together a team or group and perform a group-based estimation of user stories or features in your product backlog.

Not only are you using the technique for estimation, but the more valuable part of it, is the collaboration and conversations it creates amongst various team members. It has the effect of fostering general understanding and surfacing the implementation details of your user stories.

Every estimator gets a small deck of cards that is loosely based on the Fibonacci sequence. The cards include— Infinity, 0, ½, 1, 2, 3, 5, 8, 13, 20, 40, and 100 which represent the story points representing the size and complexity of the Story. Similar to Priority Poker, when conducting a Planning Poker estimation meeting, the flow is along the following lines:

For each User Story:

1. The Product Owner or someone closest to understanding the nature of the story explains it to the team; briefly for about 1-2 minutes.
2. The team gets a chance to ask clarifying questions of the Product Owner. I usually limit this to 5 minutes or 3-5 questions, so we don't try and over analyze the story.
3. Then everyone throws a card (at the same time, not showing their cards early) that they think represents the size of the story.
4. Then there is discussion surrounding the high and low estimates. Why did you think it was so? What were your thoughts and experiences behind the estimate? Everyone listens and engages.
5. Next, welcome additional clarifying questions.

---

[44] I believe Mike Cohn is the originator of the technique within the agile community. Certainly he has given it the broadest reference in his Agile Estimation and Planning book. He's also created a Planning Poker site that supports use of the technique for distributed teams, which is free and quite nice – http://www.planningpoker.com/

[45] Wideband Delphi predates Planning Poker. It was used in the 1980's by Barry Boehm and his Rand colleagues for traditional projects. At its core is collaborative (multi-opinion and conversation based) estimation, although with some skew towards Subject Matter Expertise (SME) contributors.

6. The goal is to discuss, then throw cards again several times until the team converges and agrees on a team based singular or ranged estimate.

Remember, these are not explicit time estimates, nor commitments for doing the work. That will come later during sprint planning. Instead, these are *High Level Story Point* estimates that should be used for ordering and planning the product backlog. As I've mentioned, they're of immense help when you're *packing* stories into sprints and performing your release planning; they give you an approximate size and relative level of effort associated with each story.

Another quick point is that they're *relative to each other*! For example, if you have a user story that's been estimated at 3 points, and one at 8 points, then the latter is roughly 2 ½ times the size of the former; independent of the numbers associated with the story points.

From a Product Owner's perspective, that's a valuable bit of information to know when making priority and value calls across Product Backlog Items.

Oh and one more important thing: ONLY those who are doing the work get a chance to play or vote. Product Owners fully engage in the collaborative process, but typically don't get a voice in the estimates. Sounds right, doesn't it?

Reference Stories

A useful technique to help your planning poker estimation is to establish a set of "reference stories" that represent the various values and types of work your team will routinely be estimating.

For example, if your team typically estimates stories at 1, 3, 5, 8, 13, 20+ values. And they do work either on front-end, UI based stories or back-end, database centric stories; they might want to capture a set of reference stories as they're estimating.

For example, the UI folks might find the perfect 1, 5, and 13 point stories and the back-end folks a different range of examples. These are real stories that were estimated by the team and then executed within a sprint. The execution turned out to be close to the original story point value, so the team did a nice job of envisioning and executing the story.

These then become _reference stories_ during backlog grooming and planning poker sessions. Whenever there is a doubt about a story's size, it is "held up against" the reference stories as a means of envisioning its size. I've often used the term 'calibration' when establishing reference stories, in that we _align or calibrate_ the story descriptions (scope) with a specific level of complexity and size (points).

Following from this, then you occasionally might need to recalibrate a team's reference stories. Quite often a new team will establish a set of reference stories when they are very new to planning poker estimation and Scrum in general. After executing a few sprints, they'll find that they've learned quite a bit and their estimation values have changed and improved. This is usually a good time to recalibrate. Caution though, you don't want to recalibrate too frequently as each time you do it; it potentially _disrupts your historical velocity values_[46].

Another wonderful side-effect of establishing reference stories is that it helps teams' consistency in their point estimation. This is particularly important in at-scale Scrum instances where you're trying to aggregate velocity across multiple teams to forecast release capacity. It is incredibly hard to do this if every team is all over the map with their point estimates. But by establishing a transparent set of _relatively consistent_ reference stories, you can guide the teams towards _relatively consistent_ estimates.

What Are You Estimating?

It's important to stress to the team that they're estimating _all_ work associated with each story into a single story point value. Sometimes this is difficult and I've worked with teams that handled it differently, based on the types of work. For example, if your application is composed of Web, Middleware, and Backend Database tiers, then you might be tempted to capture 4 story point estimates for each story. So, how do you then handle the scenario in Figure 9?

---

[46] I usually recommend that a new team runs 2-3 sprints with a baseline-guess for their estimates—normally not based on reference stories because they don't have any. Then after a few sprints, gather some reference stories and recalibrate their velocity. Leverage this for a while as they build up a solid, historical view to their velocity. Perhaps for 3-6 months if possible. Then, if there is a need to recalibrate, do it, but 'adjust' your historical velocity data based on the recalibration.

You probably don't want to recalibrate more than once every 3-6 months. Another good time to do it is when you get an influx of new team members.

Story – *Add new authentication and security checking logic to the B2B interface component*	Story Points
Web tier	3
Middle / Business Logic – tier	3
Backend DB – tier	13
Testing	8

Figure 9, Example story layers estimate

Do you add up all the estimates and use that as the overall estimate? Or take the highest one as representative of the effort? What about the distinction between development versus testing work?

Does this approach promote 'healthy' agile team behavior? Or does it foster functional silo thinking and a Waterfall-esque, throw-it-over-the-wall to the tester's mentality? What if, in this case, there was other external work by technical writers or operations groups. How would you handle those?

The estimating process can get quite complex as you try and align it against your group's functional skills structure. While I can see some contexts where this might be useful, I much prefer asking the team for a single estimate that represents the overall size and complexity of the work associated with each story – simply, *one estimate for all work*.

Not only does this make the estimation easier, but it focuses the entire team towards estimating the work to be done as a team versus the partitioned and individualistic view that the above method fosters. This approach also has a tendency for the team to round up to the greater value. Since one of our greatest weaknesses as software teams is estimation in any capacity, this isn't necessarily a bad side-effect.

Another positive side-effect of handling the estimates inclusive of all work is that it often fosters more of a swarming mentality when the team eventually gets to attacking the work. Point being, the more you compartmentalize the estimates, the more you might compartmentalize the work later in the sprint.

Wrapping Up

❖ For most Backlogs, bundle your user stories into reasonable and relevant Groups or Themed packages for most of your prioritization and workflow planning. Filling in miscellaneous stories to "fill up" your sprints.

❖ Estimate all of your stories, but emphasize that story points are **high level**, **relative**, and don't directly map to **time**; so, don't spend too much time on them. Throw an estimate and move on as you can, and should, revisit them often.

❖ The return from effective estimation is two-fold; resulting in insights into sizes for better story decomposition, as well as, planning and collaboration around story design and sprint packaging.

❖ The Fibonacci series has the intentional side-effect of "rounding up" for higher levels of points. Not only does this indicate ambiguity, complexity and larger size; but it serves as a potential reminder for the need to break them down later on.

❖ Reference stories are a wonderful way to gain consistency in your story pointing efforts. I like to print them out and hang them on the wall in the room where a team will be grooming. That way we can reference (envision) how each new story maps to our references.

Section 3

Scrum Sprint Dynamics & Execution

There are five chapters in this section focused towards the dynamics of setting up, running, and closing sprints. This is the real world with respect to Scrum teams providing business value and results.

Chapter 11 – Goal Setting at Many Levels
Goals are what 'drive' agile teams toward successful delivery of valuable and high quality software. No goals and a team can wander aimlessly. Here we explore the role the Product Owner plays in "directional clarity".

Chapter 12 – Agile Project Chartering
Many think that agile projects just start immediately sprinting towards success. Often this isn't wise or prudent. Having a map of the landscape can be incredibly useful.

Chapter 13 – Sprint Planning
Exploring key aspects of Product Owner engagement in sprint planning.

Chapter 14 – Sprint Execution
Exploring key aspects of Product Owner engagement in sprint execution.

Chapter 15 – Sprint Review: A Defining Moment!
The sprint review is one of the most compelling moments within agile iterations; the team demonstrating "working software". It can be wonderful or a disaster. Here we explore achieving the former result.

Chapter 11

Goal Setting at Many Levels

One of my greatest frustrations in coaching many agile teams is their lack of focus on goal-setting. I see many sprints that have weak and/or non-existent goals with the Product Owner coming into the planning meeting too focused on a set of stories or features and forgetting about setting a proper goal.

In my view, goal setting is one of the most important responsibilities of a Product Owner. It's how you set the stage for, and motivate your team. It's ultimately how you measure their success towards meeting your goals. Not simply by delivering some arbitrary number of stories, but driving them towards delivering cohesive themes of highly customer valued work.

It's also how you drive creativity within your agile teams. How can the team solve real problems if they're simply following your lead and are measured by a list of features? I think the point is; they can't. I contend that self-directed teams need _vision setting goals_ in order to drive their efforts, creativity, and ultimately their work.

A key component of the Product Owner's role is to collaborate with their business partners and stakeholders determining their needs; then converting those needs into a compelling strategy and set of goals that guide their teams' forward progress!

A Goal Story

I was coaching a team in their first implementation of Scrum. It was a very small, entrepreneurial start-up company that was looking for an early round of funding. They planned on demonstrating their software at a prestigious Venture Capital conference where each start-up company received six minutes to present their product idea on stage. Since the conference was on a fixed date and they had historically struggled to hit their date targets, they wanted to try something new...Scrum. Given the circumstances and implications, I cautioned them against such a risky strategy, but they were adamant.

The Sprint Goal in this case, their very first one, was to—"Create a compelling demo and stir investment interest amongst the VC's at the event". That was it. The product was a SaaS[47] software process application with a myriad of process measurement functions. However, they had six minutes to put it through some interesting paces in order to illustrate its true potential.

Their newly minted Product Owner quickly put together a series of stories that he thought were compelling and the team went and planned their first sprint.

Almost immediately these planned stories were impacted by real feature limitations and bugs in the application. As a result, the Product Owner had to make many adjustments over the initial few days—changing and fine-tuning the stories associated with the sprint. Task assignments also frequently changed, in some cases including additions and deletions.

Long story short; they derived a compelling demo story during the sprint and won significant funding. Did the original stories and tasks remain constant? No. However, the Sprint Goal was the driving constant that they measured all changes against.

In the end, the goal steered their adjustment efforts and they met the goal.

Charter – Vision & Mission

The first level of goal setting is at the overriding project or release level. I usually think of this as traditional project chartering, but with an agile flavor. It's always worthwhile for the Product Owner to sit down with their business colleagues and key stakeholders to define an overall mission and vision.

These are typically high level objectives, but ones in which you detail the _Prime Directive_ for the project or product development effort. Here's a quick example:

---

[47] SaaS – Software as a Service deliver model. Think of it as a 'hosted' solution.

Our vision is for this release to substantially change the inventory management and check-out logic in our marketplace support to improve our customer experience.

Our mission is to fix the approximately 200+ bugs in this space, re-factor the checkout UI interfaces, and improve DB performance within Inventory by a factor of 5 times.

The key benefit in setting the Vision and Mission is that it laser focuses the team about what is important at a *release* level, and should, hopefully, focus story prioritization, sprint planning, and overall team execution.

Release Goals

Release goals are another step down from the overall vision and mission. This would be a major step towards realizing the overall vision. As we move down in granularity, it's important to make your goals *as crisp as possible*[48]. There's an acronym that helps here that you've probably heard before called SMART. SMART should be a guiding model for all of your goals and criteria; making them as *smart*[49] as possible. For our sample flow, then a release goal might have the following form:

Within the next 3 development sprints, prioritize and attack the highest priority 150 defects, releasing and verifying fixes after each sprint. In addition, re-factor DB functionality within the Inventory Management Component so
that we can measure precise performance.

So, why define goals? What's the point? The answer is to measure your achievement relative to them. In this case, the team will be planning all of their work relative to the above goal. Of course, they will measure their tasks and features delivered, determining their velocity. This will give them a sense of their overall effort, their challenges, and their performance. They should ultimately be measured against how they delivered against the *goal*. This is the one thing that should be *accomplished*, with everything else being simply a means to this end.

---

[48] In the next chapter we will be exploring the notion of a Minimal Marketable / Viable Product definitions. To my way of thinking, they align nicely with release-level goals.

[49] SMART = Specific, Measurable, Achievable, Realistic, Time-boxed & Trackable

Sprint Goals

Every sprint should have a *goal*[50] and it shouldn't relate to getting specific stories done, or working hard, or making the business *happy*. Instead, each sprint should have a compelling goal that is tied to the business and stakeholder needs. It should also align with the overall vision, mission, and the release goals. Just to complete the exercise, here would be a reasonable sprint goal for the example goal sequence:

> In this sprint we're going to resolve the Top 50 bugs that are located throughout the Inventory Look-Up / Reconciliation Components and, then, resolve them. Particular attention will be paid to inconsistent data handling and adding future diagnostics for Inventory Performance monitoring.

I hope you detected the "drill down" nature of good goal setting and how they provide *cohesion* for your efforts.

Focusing Sprint Goals

I usually coach teams to think about the email they'll be sending to their organization to invite them to their sprint's review. I usually give them a headline and 2-3 sentences of real estate to describe what attendees will see. The email has to market the review, so it needs to be compelling. It also needs to be in clear English, so techno-speak.

Another way to describe it; is as an "elevator pitch" for the sprint. I think this guidance applies to crafting your sprint goals as well. They should be relatively short, express a singular, cohesive idea or focus. They should *connect* the goal to the demo and the experience the customer will have while reviewing the working software.

Anti-pattern examples of how not to craft your sprint goal would be the following:

> The goal for this sprint is to execute stories #3, 6, 17, 110, 42, and 88. We will also fix bugs 11001-11008.

---

[50] Roman Pichler wrote a nice blog post that speaks to effective sprint goals. In it he emphasizes three innovation drivers: desirability, feasibility, or viability. More on it here - http://www.romanpichler.com/blog/agile-product-innovation/effective-sprint-goals/

This was connected too much to the discreet work items and not to the customer experience. Or this,

> The goal of this sprint is to demo the dual-backup app, the look and feel for the edit engine interface, the rendering performance improvements we made, the refactoring of the PDF exporting, and, and, and...

In this case, there's no focus to the goal. It's simply a set of disparate functional additions or changes. Perhaps 2-3 would have been all right, but this is far too many. Where's the cohesion and flow? Where is the succinct customer challenge or problem that's being solved?

From who's Perspective?

It was fortuitous when I was writing this section for the second edition of this book that there was a discussion on the Certified Scrum Coaches (CSC) group surrounding sprint goals. Dan Rawsthorne, who wrote the book, <u>Exploring Scrum: The Fundamentals – People, Product, and Practices</u>, gave a few of the following example from his perspective. They are in chapter 4.2 of his book:

- **'Have a releasable version of <Buy an e-Ticket>'** – indicating that, even though the Team is *almost* there, and everybody thinks it shouldn't take much more effort, make sure you get 'Buy an e-Ticket' ready to go – even if it means reprioritizing the other Stories in the Sprint, creating Technical Debt.
- **'Clean up Module ABC'** – indicating that, even though functional Coding Stories have been agreed to, and are important, what is *really important* is cleaning up some Technical Debt.
- **'Release the Product'** – indicating that it is imperative that the Product go out the door. Do whatever it takes, including sacrificing features, quality, and work/life balance – but get it out the door.
- **'Bring the new people, Joe and Gina, up to speed'** – indicating that speed of development may be sacrificed if it helps in knowledge-sharing with the new Team Members.

- **'Be able to write 'real' code the first day of the next Sprint'** – this is common for a so-called Sprint Zero (see chapter 4.9) and indicates that the Team needs to do *enough* analysis, have *enough* development environment, have *enough* training, and so on, so that it can begin production immediately. This is used to eliminate a long, up-front, setup period.

- **'No Technical Debt in this Sprint'** – let's actually follow the rules and take no shortcuts this time, shall we?
- **'Everybody goes home by 6:00pm'** – we need to get our work/life balance back, and stop working at an unsustainable pace.
- **'Nobody works alone this Sprint'** – everybody Pairs or Swarms, let's just bite the bullet and get used to it...

One of the other coaches pointed out that these were all from the perspective of "the team" and not from "the business". There was some healthy debate, surrounding the intent of the goal, within the CSC group. Dan felt strongly that the goal was there to help the team envision their work.

And while I agree with that, I also feel his examples are too team-centric. It's truly hard to find the business value and the customer in those goals.

I'm not directly saying they're wrong and I certainly respect Dan's experience, but I don't think they align with my view of the power of sprint goals. That is: to align the team with the business and not the other way around.

The Chicken or the Egg?

In the same discussion, there was the point of what do you start and end with. So, do you start with the sprint goal and align all of the work in the sprint towards the goal? Or do you plan the sprint with the team and then derive a goal from what emerged from the sprint planning? It's a true chicken & egg problem, but I think it an important distinction.

Dan recommended the latter approach and alluded to the Scrum Guide doing that as well. Again, I almost always recommend the former approach, as follows:

1. Start with the Sprint Goal
2. Align all the teams work from the backlog towards the Goal
3. At the end of sprint planning, realign the Goal if necessary
4. Gain Product Owner and Team agreement that the Goal is SMART
5. Finally, deliver on the Goal

My central guidance surrounds leading with your goals and making them align with your customer or business needs, which perhaps makes me the chicken in the debate.

Done-Ness Criteria or Definition of Done (DoD)

I gave a talk at the 2008 Agile Conference and had the wonderful opportunity to walk around networking and learning for five whole days. One of my observations during the week was the number of presenters that emphasized _Done-Ness Criteria_ in their discussions. I'd say at least 5-8 presentations referred to them in various forms.

This aligned quite nicely with my own experience as it is absolutely critical to define multi-level goals within your agile teams. The final level of these goals should be _done-ness_, as done will need to be defined for each functional team role and for your features, in general, via acceptance tests.

At the functional level your developers, testers, and virtually all team members should decide on the work practices and steps required to actually declare a piece of work to be completed. Let's pick on developers for a second; however, the point applies to all team members. If I've developed a component and want to declare it done within my current sprint, we might want to check-off on the following:

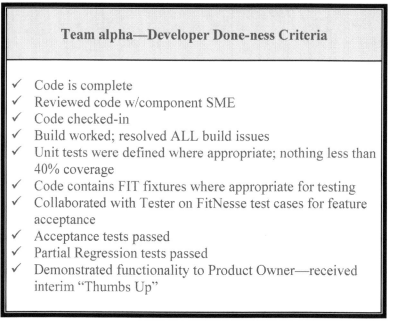

Figure 10, Sample Done-ness Criteria from a Developer Perspective

Setting solid done-ness criteria has several important benefits within your team:

- First, it helps with sprint planning and estimating since each team member has a very clear idea as to what is expected of them in performing and completing their work.
- It also helps to reinforce consistency in deliverables; setting the expectations across the entire team for their quality.
- Another benefit, as you can see in the example, it serves to reinforce solid agile collaboration across the team.

Done-ness is not typically driven solely by the Product Owner. It's more of a team initiative and agreement; along the lines of how to *professionally deliver* high quality software. However, the Product Owner clearly has a voice in the definition of, quality of, and breadth of the definition of done across the team.

Why?

Because it drives overall quality and the level has a very clear cost to the business. You have to understand, support, and be willing to pay for the costs of your definition of done. From that perspective then, you're an important contributor to 'done'.

Release Criteria

Done-ness also extends to the release level. In this case, I think of it as equivalent to old-fashioned Release Criteria, as most of us have experienced, in more traditional or Waterfall projects. Traditionally, release criteria spoke in terms of the specific requirements for achieving a release point. Factors that might be mentioned included:

- **Quality Criteria:** Focuses towards product or application quality levels that you're trying to achieve (test coverage and traceability targets, acceptable bug levels and actions, workaround guidelines, as well as, identifying the types of testing required).

- **Functional Criteria:** Illuminating the specific set of related features required to meet the customers' needs. Speaking of any tradeoffs or compromise and defining key success criteria.

- **Process Criteria:** Steps necessary to prepare the organization to properly deploy and support the customer with the release. This would include organizational, business, operational, and important software process checkpoints.

- **Performance Criteria:** Literally the performance characteristics the software must achieve (performance, minimal platform support levels, interoperability checks) prior to release.

Typically, these criteria would be established in the beginning of a project or product development effort; usually during requirement definition and project chartering. They would align with key success criteria for the project and guide decisions along the way towards the release.

In an agile context, these criteria are less encompassing and perhaps more holistic than their Waterfall cousins. However, it is helpful to define a set of criteria for each release, learning from the traditional approaches to defining them. Don't be put off by these criteria simply because of their traditional flavor. I've found it extremely helpful to drive agile releases targets with release criteria; I suspect you will too.

Johanna Rothman and I have written *articles*[51] focused on release criteria. If you're interested in further refining yours, you might want to take a look.

Wrapping-up

❖ One goal that I didn't explore in this chapter was acceptance criteria, because I feel they're much more aligned with user stories and the notion of accepting story completion with each sprint. However, they ARE an important part of the goal equation facing agile teams.

❖ Remember, agile and Scrum teams are self-directed. You don't get good results with them by telling them what to do or micro-managing their efforts. However, it's not a free-for-all. You drive results by setting GOALS at a variety of levels. I hope this chapter has given you a feel for agile goal-setting.

---

[51] www.stickyminds.com is a repository for sets of materials by Johanna and me—more so from her though. If you have an SQE Powerpass, you can access all of the content. Here's a link to an early article that Johanna wrote on Release Criteria - http://www.stickyminds.com/getfile.asp?ot=XML&id=5889&fn=SmzXDD2224file listfilename1%2Epdf .

You can also email me to request my article on Release Criteria in Better Software magazine in 2006. I've also got a presentation available on Agile-Centric Release Criteria here - http://www.rgalen.com/presentation-download/presentations/Agile%20Release%20Criteria%20v4.pdf

Chapter 12

Agile Project Chartering

What is Chartering?

In a traditional project management sense, it's a *Process* and *Artifacts* that:

- Establishes the vision state for the project
- Defines key goals and requirements
- Captures and sets customer expectations
- Defines project participants and their roles
- Defines limits and constraints
- Establishes all resource needs and overall cost targets
- Creates a high level view to the Work Breakdown Structure and schedule
- Initiates negotiation and tradeoffs
- Ultimately defines success

Another view…

A charter is a central document or a set of supporting documents that defines the purpose, nature and attributes of an about to be undertaken software project.

It is typically constructed early in the project lifecycle, hopefully before the project is staffed and the business is pushing for a delivery date. It is usually created collaboratively as a team and shared with stakeholders upon completion.

It is intended to clearly set the stage for the project; aligning the team and stakeholders by setting goals and expectations.

It's often the case that a charter leads to an early project approval 'gate' as part of an organizational project approval life-cycle phase. Usually the keys to the approval involve cost, schedule, and scope definitions and restrictions – so very much of a <u>*contractual*</u> view.

Components of an Effective Project Charter

Charter Element	Focus
Purpose	Primary rationale, compelling and clear, mission and vision for the effort
Goals	Technical, business, product, and team objectives
Scope	Customer needs, functional and non-functional requirements, bounds
Organization	Executive / stakeholder, project, functional organization structures
Resources	Space, equipment, people, skill sets and capabilities, collaboration support, tools
Approaches	Strategy, methodologies, processes, tools, and techniques
Priorities	Ordering, importance, trade-offs, relative to other projects
Assumptions and Constraints	Restrictions, limits, bounds – team, process, product, and schedule
Risks	Top 'N' risks, known, previous history, uncertainty elaborated, with mitigation plans
Sign-off	Stakeholder approval; contract nature

Figure 11, Components of an Effective Project Charter

Notion of Agile Chartering

Now let's move on from traditional chartering views to agile chartering. The essence is the same, to establish a baseline understanding and connection between the team and stakeholders. However, the dynamics and artifacts are often quite different.

First, it's not contractual in nature; resisting fixing cost, time, and scope. An agile charter clearly realizes that _scope is the variable_ within agile projects and that team's _converge_ towards their customers' needs and project goals. There's also the implication that business stakeholders are _engaged_ along the way in decision-making surrounding requisite trade-offs.

The key chartering activities, from an agile perspective, revolve around the following:

1. Establishing a view to Vision & Mission
2. Establishing a view towards a Minimum Viable Product, Minimal Marketable Product
3. Running Iteration #0's as needed; when your project and/or your team needs "directional alignment"
4. Establishing effective release plans that align the Product Backlog with the project mission, vision, and goals along with the team

We explored mission and vision a bit in the last chapter. Release planning is something we explore in much more detail in Chapter 16. For the remainder of this chapter, we're going to explore #2-3 in more detail.

Liftoff

Diana Larsen and Ainsley Nies have written an entire *book* [52] about what I'd effectively call chartering, while they coined the term Liftoff instead. The book is focused towards a triangle of sorts where they speak of connecting:

*   **Purpose**,
*   **Alignment**, and
*   **Context** as key elements in agile chartering.

Purpose is established or defined. It is mostly in the realm of your leadership team and our business stakeholders to define. In a perfect world, they establish some sort of criteria for project success.

Context is the environment in which you find yourself, for example a new or 'greenfield' project that is just beginning as a twinkle in someone's eye, or a maintenance project for a legacy system. Context would also include the team; for example, if you have a well-established or entirely new team that is new to the product domain.

---

[52] *Liftoff – Launching Agile Teams & Projects* was published in 2012. In my opinion, it's a wonderful book that compliments this one quite nicely. I'd also say it is "mandatory reading" for a Great Product Owner.

Alignment connects the two; purpose to your context. It surrounds how you do that with artifacts, meetings, explorations, prototypes, agreements; even games and ceremonies.

In my view, chartering typically surrounds purpose and alignment. Context is the situational bit that influences the decisions we make, the approaches we take, and the artifacts we create during chartering. It's the strategic thinking part.

I highly recommend Liftoff as a focused book on the notion of chartering; particularly if you're looking for collaborative tools and ideas to charter with your teams.

Minimal Marketable Feature (MMF) or

Minimal Marketable Product (MMP)

Often in agile teams, singular stories don't have sufficient mass or impact to effectively be VALUE-ated by the team or customer. Earlier in Section 2, I spoke in terms of themes of stories, which is a common way of bundling stories together that have value and meaning as a collection. Not only does it help in developing sets of meaningful functionality, but if you prioritize them at the thematic or collection level, it greatly simplifies your prioritization. It also has more meaning from the customers' perspective; since they tend to think in terms of features or workflows and not the more granular stories.

A variation on this theme (pun intended) is the Minimal Marketable Feature/Product or MMF/MMP. This concept originated in the Kanban and Lean communities. Essentially, it's the same as a theme, but it brings to bear the notion of deliverability, marketability, and overall customer usage.

Quite often an MMF/MMP is larger than a theme. It could be equivalent to a user story epic and require many sprints and/or teams to complete. However, once completed, the team will usually physically deliver the MMF/MMP to the customer—for example, pushing it into a production environment.

MMF Driving Synchronization and Clarity

Recently, I've been coaching teams that are struggling with their focus. There's an anti-pattern that affects many teams where they start sprinting before they understand the business case and intent for their release(s).

They're delivering stories, but they don't necessarily understand the minimal set of functionality that their customers are looking for.

Not having this clearly articulated up-front becomes a fundamental problem for them. Quite often their customers have an expectation of delivery that is quite different from what the team is sprinting towards delivering. Consequently, there's no collaborative clarity around what the MMF or MMP is between the team, stakeholder(s), and customer(s).

One nice way to connect the two back together is to establish a view towards the releases' MMF. Part of defining the MMF is the round-trip discussions that occur as the teams estimate and/or size up the stories and features within the MMF. The customer reevaluates whether they truly need that functionality given the investment of time. This collaboration dove-tails quite nicely into release planning, discussed in Chapter 16, as the team narrows into fitting the MMF into a specific release window.

I've even seen multiple sorts of MMF's developed for release planning—for example, a UX MMF that tries to capture usability and interaction flows vs. the cost of implementing them. Or, similarly, an Architecture / Refactoring MMF that tries to guide these sorts of trade-offs.

MMF or MMP Simplicity

When a team is defining their minimal marketable feature or product, I want it to fit on a single sheet of paper. I'm looking for the elevator pitch or 'essence' of the product to be described.

I often ask for what needs to be in the product to be defined, but also what doesn't need to be in the product. Occasionally, I use a "What's IN versus What's OUT" chart to get the point across. It defines the must haves and the must not haves for the MMF (or MMP). It turns out the crucial part of the chart is the gray area in between these two dimensions and the discussions that surround understanding the *minimal set of functionality*[53].

Often features will move back and forth. Features will get broken down and some aspects move from one column or the other or they are removed entirely. Let me give you an example to help illustrate this concept. If we

---

[53] It turns out that organizations and teams truly struggle with focusing on a Must Have set of functionality. The Minimal Marketable () construct helps quite a lot in keeping the focus…minimal.

were doing a simple collaborative white-boarding tool for agile teams, the following example in Figure 12 might be a reasonable MMP definition to start discussions across your team.

MMF Must Have (Black)	Collaborative Grey Area	MMF Will Not Have (White)
• Visual swim lanes – vertical & horizontal • Create notes (colors) • Drag & drop notes • Shape library • Drawing tool • Multiple users collaborate on a board • Save/recall a board • Identify board participants • Default boards for Scrum & Kanban		• Board item export • Any integration with other tools • Cut & paste • Save in common file formats • Interact with board users directly (ex: text or comment) • Performance doesn't matter

Figure 12. Example of What's IN vs. What's OUT chart

Caution: There is Minimum. Then there is Viable

There's a wonderful Harvard Business Review *blog article* [54] where David Aycan discusses additional nuances associated with the notion of an MMF. He makes the point that quite often today, in our fervor to hit the 'minimum', we over-simplify features and products and lose customer and business viability.

I haven't seen this pattern that much myself; I usually see the reverse, or teams incessantly trying to build "too much". But, he connects it to Eric Ries's Lean Startup work and I have been around enough people who are passionate about those ideas that I can see it happening. Regardless, I'd recommend you read his post.

I think the key is for us to focus on *minimal and viable* as much as possible when we're framing reactions to our customers' needs.

---

[54] http://blogs.hbr.org/cs/2012/05/dont_let_the_minimum_win_over.html

Finally, a Trip to MoSCoW

MoSCoW prioritization is a technique for breaking requirements, or stories & features, down into four specific categories for consideration, discussion, and execution. They are:

- **Must Haves** – will not release without these features and capabilities being present
- **Should Haves** – high priority features
- **Could Haves** – moderate priority, fit in if time allows, but deferrable
- And **Won't Haves** – features negotiated out of this release

When prioritizing your backlog, it helps to place these four 'buckets' on a wall or table and to visually discuss and move stories around from one to the other.

Many groups come up with some sort of ratio that helps with this. For example, out of 100 stories, perhaps only 10-20% should effectively be Must Haves and 20-30% might be valid Should Haves. This gives you some general guidance on how to compose stories into an MMF or, more often, an MMP definition.

You might want to try Moscow as a facilitative technique when you're prioritizing. My experience is that it helps to drive discussion and encourages the team to wrestle with truly "must haves" versus everything else.

Leveraging an Iteration #0

In his book on *Agile Project Management*[55], Jim Highsmith introduced the concept of running an Iteration #0.The same notion has been referenced within Scrum as Sprint #0. It is certainly NOT a core practice of Scrum as defined in the Scrum Guide. It's also somewhat of a debated practice in the Scrum community.

---

[55] Agile Project Management is a wonderful book by Jim Highsmith that speaks to the general practices surrounding Agile PM without strong ties to any specific Agile Methodology. I've found his guidance surrounding Chartering, Agile Iterative Planning, and Iteration Types to be quite useful.

The primary pushback seems to be against having sprints that don't produce "working code" as the primary or only deliverable.

Some think that for all project work, you should "dive into" your first sprint and immediately begin delivering customer value, which could include charter elements. If that's truly possible, then I couldn't agree more. In that case, you must have a clear backlog, a team formed and equipped, and a clear charter. So, why not dive in and start sprinting?

But what if things aren't so clear?

What if you have a new, never-been-together before team? Or, have moved members together into a new space and need to setup equipment? Or, they are embarking on a new project with no backlog requirements or context? Or, you are being told to use a highly distributed team to get the work done? Or, your team doesn't have much Scrum experience among them, and you've just hired a brand new Scrum Master? Or, the list goes on…

I can think of many contexts where beginning a sprint without sufficient definition can lead to nothing productive or even agile. It's just moving without a direction in mind, which can lead to chaos and churn.

In these cases, wouldn't it be useful to take a sprint, or even two, to _figure things out_? At least, to get enough definition and clarity so you can begin to sprint effectively; getting your feet underneath you? Well, that's exactly the point behind the Iteration #0.

You'll want it to behave as closely to the same dynamics as a normal, development-driven sprint; the primary compromise usually being on delivering working software in the end. You might even want to keep the sprint shorter to keep it more focused, and not run the risk of it turning into a crutch for _Waterfall analysis paralysis_[56].

---

[56] Analysis Paralysis is a term common within Waterfall projects where teams fall into a practice of nearly infinitely belaboring requirements and design and avoiding implementing software. I've personally been involved with projects that fell into the anti-pattern for months on end. This is one of the reasons I'm so drawn to the agile methods and why I have such a laser focus on getting to "Working Software" ASAP!

Typical activities that I've seen within Iteration #0's include:

- Chartering; and connecting it to your stakeholders.
- Defining your high-level architecture or connections to a pre-existing Enterprise level system or other architectures.
- Do a bit of prototyping; perhaps paper at first.
- Running story writing workshop(s) and other meetings / activities to establish your initial Product Backlog.
- Running backlog grooming meeting(s) to provide initial Product Backlog Item estimates and perform release planning.
- Forming your team: introductions, establishing roles, assessing skills, etc.
- Establishing a working environment for your team: Scrum room, cubes, workstations, development and test tool servers, connections to existing tools, etc.
- Running various training sessions for your team; both technical, Scrum, and team related.
- Perhaps conducting a project kick-off of sorts.
- Planning for, then kicking off your first sprint; then off you go…

One of the dangers associated with the Iteration #0, and I've already alluded to it, is that teams who are uncomfortable with ambiguity, can begin using it as an excuse for analysis paralysis. They may even want the *false comfort of too much early definition*. Therefore, you'll want to be careful that you schedule them when they are truly needed, and only continue them as long as that strong need exists.

For example, I've never seen a large-scale or enterprise-level project that needed more than 2 – 2-week Iteration #0's to get their feet underneath them before actively sprinting.

Re-running Your Iteration #0

I view Iteration #0's as a potential "iterative wrapper" for agile project chartering. You typically think of it as occurring at the beginning of a project, but that's not the only appropriate time. Many agile teams get into a state of what I refer to as "directional confusion" in alignment towards feasibly meeting their goals. Re-chartering can help those teams realign themselves with their business stakeholders.

Another factor influencing this is design ambiguity. Agile teams attempt to balance architecture and design allowing them to emerge as teams iterate their solutions. But that shouldn't imply there isn't in-advance design and architectural activity within a release sequence. When a team runs out of their architectural and design look-ahead, and starts to realize more and more rework, it might be time to run another Iteration #0 to gain some design look-ahead or runway for subsequent sprints.

Point being; don't be reluctant to re-run an Iteration #0 when you find the teams encountering too much ambiguity or churn in their direction. It might only take a day or two, to regain your directional certainty and then continue with your adjusted release plans.

Exploratory 360°

Alistair Cockburn's Crystal Methodology [57] has an interesting technique that links to an Iteration #0 which I'll simply mention here. The notion is to plan an execution step to, more or less, establish your *capability* to do what you're planning to do; before you begin doing it in earnest. In other words – demonstrating that you can: "walk your talk".

For example, we often make assumptions that we have all the technical skills to perform our projects. What if we were planning on developing a website, but had no performance testing experience on our team? Moreover, the project was tight for time, had some relatively aggressive requirements for performance, and the testers assigned to the team kept saying: "Don't worry about it." As you can see, it's clearly a risky skill gap. But how do you handle it?

If you ran an Exploratory 360° as part of your preparation, then you'd be asking the testing team to perform some rudimentary performance testing on an existing application to get a feel for their capabilities. Clearly, surfacing whether they have the tools and expertise to do what you need them to do later on in the project.

This is the essence of it: from a risk surfacing perspective, ask your team to try some of the *hard bits* early so you can detect where the skill and capability gaps might be. After that, you'll be in a much better position to

---

[57] Crystal hasn't evolved to be a mainstream Agile Methodology. However, I find many of the techniques to be useful outside of its context and within the other methodologies. This is one of them. I've also heard this technique referred to as a Hudson's Bay Start, referenced here - http://www.striderandcline.com/hudsons.shtml so it's not solely an agile technique.

know where your teams' skills realistically stand and, if necessary, be able to plan for risk and mitigation actions.

Wrapping Up

❖ Chartering is more than a set of documents or pausing at the beginning of a project. It's truly about alignment between the team and their business stakeholders.

It's about when the team gets done with a release, and delivers it to their 'client', the client is delighted with the result. It meets their expectations, as they were codified in the initial chartering phases of the project.

❖ I've continued to be amazed at how powerful the notion of "Minimal Marketable" is within the context of establishing expectations. Not only when you're initially chartering, but when you're realigning your direction via re-chartering. Focus on the IN vs. OUT charts and negotiating items across the "gray area".

❖ Don't be reluctant to execute an Iteration #0. In my way of thinking, it is the iterative wrapper under which one charters. And if you need to re-charter or get your feet underneath you again during a release sequence, don't be afraid to run another Iteration #0.

That being said, please don't allow the Iteration #0 to become a device for BDUF or other up front Waterfall practices!

Chapter 13

Sprint Planning

Great Product Owners take the sprint planning meeting very seriously. They realize that, while agility isn't necessarily about planning, it is extremely important to start each sprint properly! I've been part of some of the *ugliest* sprint planning meetings imaginable. Planning meetings where the Product Owner arrived with a set of stories that hadn't been properly vetted with the team. Others where the team hadn't participated in backlog grooming, so they were totally unprepared for the meeting.

In all cases, the meetings took forever, were frustrating, sometimes needed to be cancelled and then rescheduled. It clearly set the wrong tone for the upcoming sprint. In all cases, these issues could easily have been avoided by simple pre-meeting planning.

Typical Dynamics

The *Scrum Guide* [58] describes the sprint planning meeting in the following fashion:

> The work to be performed in the Sprint is planned at the Sprint Planning Meeting. This plan is created by the collaborative work of the entire Scrum Team.
>
> The Sprint Planning Meeting is time-boxed to eight hours for a one-month Sprint. For shorter Sprints, the event is proportionately shorter. For example, two-week Sprints have four-hour Sprint Planning Meetings.
>
> The Sprint Planning Meeting consists of two parts, each one being a time-box of one half of the Sprint Planning Meeting duration. The two parts of the Sprint Planning Meeting answer the following questions, respectively:

---

[58] Scrum Guide, October 2011 version, excepts from page 9
http://www.scrum.org/Scrum-Guides

- What will be delivered in the Increment resulting from the upcoming Sprint?
- How will the work needed to deliver the Increment be achieved?

I often refer to the two parts as Part A and B of the meeting; they refer to them as Parts 1 and 2 in the Scrum Guide.

Part A is the domain of the Product Owner. In it, you should focus on relaying the sprint goal(s) and describing the theme, feature, or story set that you have targeted for this sprint. This is not the time for changing your mind or focus. Instead, you should confidently present the contents, the business priority and value, and then, address any clarifying questions the team may have. Often I refer to this as the _body of work_ that you want the team to complete during the sprint.

Once the team has a solid, high level understanding of where they're going, the meeting shifts to ***Part B***, or sprint backlog (task) planning. While the Product Owner is fully engaged in this part as well, the second half of the meeting is really for the team. It's where they perform task breakdowns for each story or Product Backlog Item, contemplating design and dependency details, then distribute work amongst the team for the sprint.

Outcomes are an important measure for planning; the team should exit sprint planning with the following minimal set of artifacts and/or understandings:

- A Sprint Goal that is clear, measurable, compelling and one that everyone understands & supports.
- A set of committed product backlog items or stories that align with the Sprint Goal(s).
- Every team member has time clearly committed to the sprint (preferably near 100% of their individual capacity, but minimally with a declared capacity).
- A set of tasks associated with each story estimated at a relatively fine level of granularity.
- Work clearly identified for each team member for, at least, the first day of the sprint.

While I realize that this list might seem daunting, the true goal is for the team to come out of the meeting with understanding of and a commitment to a body of work. And with a general game plan on how they plan on attacking that work.

Here's how the **Scrum Guide** [59] articulates the exit conditions for sprint planning:

> By the end of the Sprint Planning Meeting, the Development Team should be able to explain to the Product Owner and Scrum Master how it intends to work as a self-organizing team to accomplish the Sprint Goal and create the anticipated Increment.

A Diversion: Task Granularity

One of the major variations in many agile teams is how they attack sprint or iteration planning. I prefer that tasks are broken down into hours, but not too finely grained; so no smaller than 4 hours and no larger than 2-3 days on average. I've seen other ends of this spectrum used as well, sometimes working and more often not.

Estimating in 1-4 hour increments for tasks seems to create a false sense of comfort and understanding. I consider these tasks too finely grained; which can lead to exhaustive planning meetings.

Estimating in units of 3-5+ days implies too coarse a level of granularity and prevents appropriate team visibility in getting the work done. Also, it often introduces risk because team members aren't completing tasks quickly enough; moving them to a 'done' state. It can lead to *90% done syndrome* where nothing, or very little, actually gets completed by sprints' end.

As I've said, I prefer the guideline of tasking being in the *4 hour to 2-3 day range*[60]. This seems to give the right balance in planning visibility without micro-managing the work.

---

[59] Scrum Guide, October 2011 version, excepts from page 10
http://www.scrum.org/Scrum-Guides

[60] I usually ask beginner-level or new teams to estimate in ½ day chunks between ½ day to 3 days for their tasks. I'm trying to get them out of the weeds of 'hours' to start off. I'm also trying to get them to break things down. Once they mature, I'm fine with hourly task estimation. Consider the ½ day chunks a version of XP's Ideal Days in time accounting. More on that here:

Another Diversion: The 'Point' of Sprint Planning

I'm going to say something that may be contrary to your experience or counterintuitive, but my experience holds it to be true. The tasks defined in sprint planning really don't matter a great deal. Instead, they are simply a means to an end; that is forming a game plan for the sprint.

The stories for a sprint matter a bit more than the tasks, but aren't the whole point either. They map to the sprint goal and the demonstration plans.

What really matters is that the team has a _Sprint Goal_ and signs-up to meet it by delivering a _body of work_ that supports it. That is the _Prime Directive_ for each and every sprint.

At some level, it doesn't matter how many tasks or stories there are, nor their estimates for effort, or who has, or has not, signed up for them. Sure, having elicited them has some value from the perspective of giving the team an initial road-map for the sprint. But, what if they need to make many adjustments to achieve the sprint goal? Do we throw out the goal because of the change in game plan? Of course not!

The crucial point here is related to focus. Should the team simply focus at a task and story level, getting them individually done or, should they focus their energy towards the goal. I've always seen much improved sprint delivery performance when focused towards the latter.

So the point of sprint planning is:

1. To share and gain the team's commitment toward the sprint goal;
2. To identify the set of stories that aligns with and is feasible to deliver within the sprint;
3. To identify the tasks associated with delivering those stories.

Clearly, in that priority order and leading to _goal-driven work_[61].

---

http://blog.extremeplanner.com/2006/11/agile-estimating-how-long-is-ideal-day.html

[61] To amplify this point, I usually ask the entire Scrum team to go "Thumbs up/down" as part of committing to the sprint goal at the end of sprint planning. I won't 'exit' the meeting until we get consensus that the sprint is 'doable' and all Thumbs Up for team commitment.

Sprint Planning Adjustments

I often find that sprint planning time can be exaggerated and that optimizations are possible without compromising the quality of the meeting. A couple of points come to mind when making adjustments to your sprint planning meetings, which we'll explore next.

Shorter Sprints and Meetings

I prefer shorter, more focused planning sessions. Part of the dynamics surrounding this is to have shortened sprint lengths and smaller teams. I try to keep most sprints to about 2 weeks in length and think optimum team size is 5 +/-2, instead of the 7 +/- 2 that is often referenced. Therefore, if you have smaller iterations and teams, you should be able to shorten the meetings significantly.

The other dynamic is your preparation. I'm convinced, because I've seen it done so often, that you can conduct a complete sprint planning meeting (*Parts A and B*) in 2-3 hours for a 2-week sprint, IF you've properly vetted the backlog and have a small, focused team.

Taking Too Long

If your team finds itself spinning their wheels in a sprint planning meeting, as the Product Owner you should take primary responsibility for it. Clearly, the team isn't familiar enough with or prepared to do the work. Rather than sitting around and debating approaches and feature nuances, it's probably more congruent to cancel the meeting to figure out the appropriate next steps offline.

That same logic applies if you simply exceed your time-box for the meeting. Check in with your team and Scrum Master at this point. I've, at times, run a mini-retrospective with the team to determine where we lost our planning focus and to discuss how to get things back on track.

Distributed Sprint Planning

In some cases, you may have a distributed Scrum team working on your backlog. This can be an effective relationship if you spend time to include remote team members all backlog vetting and collaboration surrounding backlog preparation.

There are certain Scrum activities that I feel all team members need to participate in regardless of locale. Sprint planning is one of those activities.

No matter how challenging or difficult, remote team members need to be included in the meeting. I've seen tools like web cams, wiki's, Google Docs, and Skype be useful in pulling teams together. There are also mature, enterprise-level agile tools that can be of immense help in these scenarios.

Distributed Team Story

I encountered a team that was virtually split across two sites: one in Richmond, Virginia and the other in Atlanta, Georgia. Fortunately, both teams were in the same time zone making working together that much easier.

They had experimented with a variety of ways to connect the two sites effectively for agile collaboration. When I happened upon them as a coach, they had settled on the following:

They setup two physical planning boards in both locales that represented their plans and progress for each Sprint. They had also setup a webcam in each location. Each webcam was fixed on the planning boards and team areas so each group could see what was happening on the "other side".

In addition, they chose to keep a conference call line open. Initially, just for meetings: daily scrum, grooming, reviews, etc., but later on, all of the time. The reason they shared for this was that it created a tighter coupling between the groups in that each could continuously hear conversations from the other location.

They spoke of gaining the ability to sense when a remote discussion affected someone locally, and simply turning their attention to the phone to join the discussion. This gave them the feeling of physically being together, by being able to overhear and engage in appropriate discussions.

During sprint planning, each side took ownership of posting ALL cards on their respective planning walls. It happened quite naturally and every team member participated in asking questions, writing, and posting. Again, it "felt" like a single team.

I found the simplicity and effectiveness of the team's solution to be quite remarkable.

Wrapping Up

❖ Pre-vetting each backlog user story or Product Backlog Item at least 3 times will help to ensure your team is properly prepared for sprint planning and execution. First, when it's initially created; second, when it's within 2-3 Sprints of execution; and finally, when it's about to be implemented within the next sprint. Each successive drill-down provides additional clarity (descriptiveness, acceptance tests, team understanding) and better decomposition of each story.

❖ Try to help the team focus on the sprint goal first, then on stories, and finally on tasks. They'll try to go too far into the details for comfort, but keep them focused on the goal and then collaboration around the details. There's a false desire in software development for 100% clarity, which is never achieved before we begin doing the actual work. Ambiguity is something we need to become comfortable with and deal with iteratively.

❖ Never push your team too hard to cut their estimates. Teams can be quite sensitive to Product Owner pressure, both direct and more subtle and, therefore, cut estimates in order to *"please the business"*. This will ALWAYS come back to haunt you. Instead, engage in understanding by asking good questions and careful listening. Always remind the team of the quality levels required – in order to be clear about NOT trading off Quality over Time!

Chapter 14

Sprint Execution

As a Product Owner, it's quite easy to disengage during sprint execution because it seems as if your role gets somewhat diminished. You feel like the team is rolling along with work and you are only there to help when asked a question.

From my point of view, this is another area that can be a differentiator for a great Product Owner. That being said, what does a Product Owner do during the sprint?

Sprint Engagement

First of all, you need to fully engage with the team. Attend _all_ daily stand-ups and listen intently to what's going on. Look for opportunities to collaborate with the team each and every day. Are there testers you can sit down with to define and/or refine acceptance tests? Are there any stories or features approaching a demonstration state? If so, sit down with those team members and give them some early feedback. How about bugs surfacing that may need your judgment and attention? The list of activities goes on.

Remember, too, that you're a team member, so speak to your own efforts in the daily stand-up. Share your tasks, efforts, plans for that day, conversations you've had with stakeholders, etc.

Sitting with Your Team

I prefer it when Product Owners are co-located with their teams. There is no replacement for listening in on the activity; conversations, pairing, design debates, questions, comments, bugs, problems or impediments, and just being there engaging naturally and immediately, when and where you're needed within the team.

However, in some cases this is just not possible. So, the onus is on you to look for alternative strategies to support your team. Some examples include:

- If you're out of the office, dial-into all stand-ups or relevant meetings even while you're traveling.

- Establish a notion of *office hours*, where you're available for the team; I've seen an hour or two in the morning and afternoon as quite effective approaches.
- You can delegate your responsibilities, as a whole or subset, but ensure your team knows you're doing it; the details, for how long, etc. and who is representing you and in what capacity
- Even if you're remote or out of the office, regularly reach out to your team and ask if you can help; let everyone know you're available, engaged, and that you care!

I guess the point here is that <u>*being present*</u>, even when you're not physically there, is incredibly important to you, your team and the ultimate sprint outcomes. Stay committed to engagement and your team will sense it and respond in-kind.

Testing

In many teams the Product Owner is in a wonderful position of understanding customer needs and expectations, both at the story and goal levels. Given that, and their need to understand sprint progress, I usually find Product Owners spending considerable time testing their application.

Usually, they're working with the test team and on test-focused environments so that the software is, more often than not, a bit more mature. At regular intervals, they're checking on feature interaction and workflow; considering overall customer experience and usability of features being delivered within the sprint.

Time and again they'll have questions and, as a result, the testing will drive healthy collaboration from the Product Owner towards the team. They're also heavily collaborating with testers on the individual story acceptance test requirements and, if using *ATDD oriented tools*[62], they're crafting their own acceptance tests for automated execution.

The key point is that testing is a natural extension of the Product Owner role and a great way to contribute to your team's efforts in a visible and high impact way. I'd really encourage this to be a part of your focus within each sprint.

---

[62] See Appendix A for more information on Acceptance Test Driven Development or ATDD in general.

Impediments

As impediments emerge that relate to you, don't wait for the Scrum Master to track you down for follow-up action. Instead be proactive in moving all of your personal impediment actions forward. Show the team you care by the sheer level of your attention and impediment resolution focus.

Also, stay aware of sprint progress via your sprint burndown charts and other team *Information Radiators*[63]. Stay curious; ask questions of the team about work progress and challenge them if you feel work is falling behind their goal commitment. If they're ahead of the sprint plan, certainly prepare additional work that they can pull into the sprint.

If you find that a sprint is in jeopardy and the team is falling behind, get engaged with your Scrum Master and team to figure out how you can adjust sprint contents and still meet the sprint goal. Be willing to listen to *all* alternatives for changing sprint scope, but still achieve your goals. Stay open minded. In fact, proactively suggest adjustments yourself.

I call this activity making micro-adjustments to the contents of a sprint. Every adjustment should be aligned with the goal. And the adjustments happen in "both directions", based on positive and negative discovery.

Bugs

During the course of all software development, bugs arise. It's simply natural. In the case of Scrum and other Agile Methodologies, you want to try and resolve and/or fix all bugs as soon as they're discovered. Your team will need your help in deciding what are valid and immediate bugs versus what can be deferred. While maintaining a "Lean – Fix it now" mindset, help lead your team forward with balanced decision-making.

You should also be asking questions and reaffirming the quality levels of their work. I've seen many Product Owners that focus on delivering features, over delivering *high quality* features. You want to be a champion of the latter, and motivate the team towards this by asking quality-oriented questions. For example – "How could this set of bugs been avoided?" or, "What can we do to improve overall product quality?" This sets the tone that

---

[63] I believe Alistair Cockburn coined the term (Information Radiator) in his Crystal and Agile approaches books. An information radiator is literally any progress or state graphic that is placed in a team room for the team to view and react to. Consider them as a car dashboard, with the emphasis on reaction and adjustments.

you're equally committed to quality as you are to production, which is an extremely important message for your team to *continuously* hear!

An Engagement Story

If you remember, I told a story in Chapter 11 about a start-up team that used their first Scrum sprint to target a venture capital funding event. As it turns out, their first sprint also had a nice example of Product Owner engagement.

As you may recall, this was their very first sprint. I had come in to give them a few hours of training, helped them craft an initial Product Backlog, facilitated a sprint planning meeting and assisted them with the kick-off of their first sprint; all in a matter of a few days. Obviously, even though they were truly inexperienced, they were also extremely motivated and focused on their goal.

About one week into their 4-week sprint, while I was traveling, I received a call from their Product Owner, at 5 a.m. (PST) regarding their burndown chart. It seemed that they were not burning down as expected and it appeared as if they weren't going to make their goal. However, when challenged on their progress, the team spoke of dependencies and how things were actually nicely on-track. I suggested that he continue to probe his team, and wait a few days; trusting their guidance.

When they did get the burndown to represent their real progress a few days' later, things were much better aligned. However, it appeared like they would only get about 80% of their stories completed. This was a real problem given the fact that additional VC funding was riding on their overall story content.

The very next day, the Product Owner gave me a call (again, 5 a.m. PST), but hey... he had a sprint progress observation and wanted my advice. He said it seemed clear that the team was going to miss delivering some of the features for the sprint. However, he was OK with that and wanted to know if he could start removing or reframing stories in order to increase the team's ability to meet the sprint goal?

In other words, could he make some minor scope micro-adjustments within the sprint? Here's a Product Owner who, in their very first Sprint, gets the difference between <u>planned scope</u> versus <u>actual team capacity</u> and the need for ongoing, real-time adjustments.

Additionally, based on internal demonstrations, he wanted to know if he could change some story characteristics to make their overall demo more powerful; thus better supporting the sprint goal. I said sure! Work with your team and figure out the requisite changes to have an outrageously successful funding demo. The sooner, the better!

It seemed this Product Owner <u>got</u> the whole Scrum customer engagement model and dynamically worked with his team to adjust, based on progress discovery and feedback, on how to creatively and realistically create a compelling demo. To complete the story, the team successfully garnered their funding.

Even more compelling to me was how immediately and well the Product Owner engaged an agile mindset with his team. Now, that's a Product Owner on the verge of greatness!

Adjusting the Sprint?

As the previous story indicated, sprints quite often don't turn out as planned and something needs to be adjusted in the middle of things. One reason might be to make priority changes, based on external customer changes to the content of the sprint. Another is when the team finds itself struggling with their original commitment to the work; if they either under or overestimated things. And another reason is that software is by definition a challenging endeavor and, therefore, sometimes unexpected risks may surface. We're going to explore a few scenarios here.

One important point is that none of these actions are solely the responsibility of the Product Owner. In fact, the leader here should be the Scrum Master. He or she is your partner and should guide you and the team in making any necessary adjustments, etc. However, you do play a significant part in what I'll call the sprint *recovery* process.

Content Disconnect

The team is struggling to deliver to their sprint commitment. Within the first few days of the sprint, you and the Scrum Master realize that an adjustment is necessary. I've seen several approaches to this. Classically, Scrum allows for cancelling and re-planning your Sprint. That works well if you're a stand-alone team. However, if your team is synchronized with others, then this approach can be awkward in that you'll need to plan a reduced length sprint in order to maintain your cross-team synchronization.

Another approach is to simply run a re-planning meeting or what I call a "soft reset". This is where the team, given the recent discoveries, tries to maximize delivery of content towards the original sprint goal. Since you're using the previous sprint backlog as a baseline, this is usually a quick meeting where you and the team figure out an adjusted game plan for the sprint.

If done quickly enough, within the first 1-3 days of a two week sprint, I've seen teams significantly recover their progress and often meet the original sprint goal. If detected too late, then you're simply trying to maximize the deliver towards the goal; not meeting the goal itself.

Capacity or Focus Disconnect

Let's face it; we live in the real world where interruptions are incredibly common and dynamic. For example, if a Severity 1 bug surfaces at a customer site, rarely is it the right answer to tell them that they'll have to wait until the end of the sprint.

Or if you have one database architect for ten Scrum teams, rarely is it the right answer to have them focus on one team over the others. Interruptions happen and multi-tasking isn't entirely avoidable. That being said, it can be incredibly demoralizing to a Scrum team to have their sprints derailed with interruptions.

When it happens you want to immediately discuss the impact with the team and re-plan the sprint; trying to maintain the sprint goal as much as possible. But beyond the current sprint, try to put some thought into how the team can mitigate similar situations in future sprints, for example:

- Reserving time (capacity) for external interruptions.
- Allocating a team member to be the 'buffer' for external interruptions.
- Planning on less work within the sprint; yes, that's not a typo—I really said that.
- Raising an impediment for specific team skills in order to effectively execute the backlog.
- Capturing interruption time during the sprint as 'drag' or interrupt time to be better able to quantify the impacts.

Priority Disconnect

One of my favorite Product Owners struggled with changing his mind quite often within sprints. We were working on an eCommerce SaaS (Software as a Service) application where "things changed" often due to customer and market dynamics. In these cases, he was more likely to cancel the sprint and then re-plan a new one based on a major priority shift in the backlog.

However, when re-planning we tried to stay open minded about integrating the new work and maintaining some of the original sprints' focus. This lessened the teams' feelings of getting "jerked around".

Another aspect of this is insufficient look-ahead. I was never convinced that he couldn't anticipate these changes in some way. Remember, we were on a 2-week sprint model which is fairly nimble. As we'll discuss next, looking ahead and anticipating events is another important activity during sprint execution.

Looking Ahead

Another place to invest time with your team and each sprint is *"looking ahead"* in anticipation of future actions. For example:

- Ensure the team reserves time during each sprint for backlog grooming activity. Then, actively schedule backlog grooming and estimation meetings as required.
- Actively work with Stakeholders to anticipate changes; then factor them into the backlog for future sprints and releases. Make it HARD to interrupt ongoing sprints.

- Examine the team's velocity within the sprint, also considering past sprint velocity. If they're going to have problems delivering in this sprint, get engaged in making appropriate adjustments.
- Adjust the backlog based on velocity versus delivered value versus release plans versus your budget. Always remember, it's a dynamic list!
- Remind team members to add, change, break down, combine, and remove items from the backlog; to proactively manage it with you.
- Potentially remove items from the Backlog that may be too large, too future oriented, lack relevancy or, in general, dilute the team's attention.
- Getting the backlog stories ready for execution within the next sprint and developing a new sprint goal.
- If you're working in an environment with multiple Scrum teams and cross-backlog dependencies, ensure you collaborate across the Product Owner organization.

These are all activities that you should be engaging in with your team.

Preparing for the Sprint Review

During the sprint, you should also be monitoring progress on a story-by-story basis and mapping progress to the overall burndown chart to get a feel whether the sprint will be successful or not; in other words, preparing for the sprint review. One of the core tenants of agility is delivering and demonstrating *working software* which should happen in Scrum in the sprint review.

Wrapping Up

❖ Remain fully engaged in the sprint and attend all daily Scrum meetings. Listen to the "progress pulse" from the team, and always be ready to make adjustments, while looking for opportunities where you might be able to help. Sitting with your team during the sprint can make a huge difference.

❖ Get involved with all aspects of "Testing the App" within the sprint. You're not only testing; you're providing wonderful feedback and helping your team.

❖ "Look ahead" as much as possible within the sprint towards future sprints. Engage the team in backlog grooming and estimation meetings and/or activities; this will help avoid the sprint-by-sprint vision that undermines many teams' potential.

Chapter 15

Sprint Review: A Defining Moment!

Transparency is certainly one of the keys to effective performance of your agile teams. One of the best Scrum mechanisms for exposing your team's results is the sprint review. It supports some of the basic tenants of agility by:

Demonstrating working software (potentially shippable product increment) to your Customer and gaining their acceptance of your work.

The sprint review really is a defining moment for the team and the place where value is demonstrated. It shouldn't be construed as a simplistic marketing or contrived demonstration of software that may crash at any moment. Instead, the software features should be robust and well behaved.

It's not necessarily highly polished. I've seen *FitNesse test*[64] demonstrations (fixtures, test cases, execution) that weren't very powerful or slick. However, they contained tremendous value from a business and quality perspective and we endeavored to get that point across. Incidentally, we executed the tests during the sprint review.

Even though the sprint review is a holistic team event, I would like to share a few focus points that Product Owners can, and should, bring to the table for a powerful and defining moment to conclude each and every sprint.

Taking Ownership for Attendance

It's crucial that you get the right business stakeholders and other interested parties in the sprint review. It's important from a team morale perspective, from a transparency perspective, and it's also important from a feedback perspective.

I've seen a common pattern where attendance is spotty in reviews. Sometimes there is good engagement and, at other times not. Every so often, we would send out the meeting invitations late, even though it's a regularly

---

[64] See Appendix A for more information.

scheduled event tempo and this would drastically affect attendance. Or, we wouldn't effectively explain what was on the agenda for the review. Where sometimes customer-facing colleagues who would find great value in the review, aren't included or don't attend. Often times, if key participants can't attend, they also neglected to send an advocate or a delegate.

All of these symptoms indicate a lack of preparation and engagement on the part of the Product Owner. The sprint review is the _defining moment_ for the team's work, including your own, at the end of each sprint. It is absolutely unacceptable to do a poor job of getting the right people there; on time and excited about the possibilities.

I have no _special tricks_ [65] to provide, nor silver bullets, simply the council to take ownership of attendance – to take it seriously. Personally invite participants, preferably face-to-face and then by follow-up email. Follow-up if they don't attend. I'd even go so far as to say it's an _impediment_ if attendance is poor on a regular basis and would consider it an indicator that the project lacks business value and importance.

Keys to Inspire Review Attendance

Here is a selection of ideas for initiating and keeping folks coming to your teams' sprint reviews:

- Schedule the reviews at a reoccurring time synchronized with your sprints. The more teams that can meet during the time-slot, the easier for stakeholders to carve out the time.
- Pull a detailed agenda together for each review and publish it early. Speak to what the team(s) will show in customer-oriented, clear English language.
- Show more "working software", and less PowerPoint's.

---

[65] While it's not a special trick, I'd suggest you ask key stakeholders and customers why they're not attending and work with your Scrum Master and team to adjust as much as possible to their feedback. Another idea is to schedule sprint reviews only when there's something significant to demonstrate. I see this problem in teams with shorter sprint cycles, say 1-2 weeks. It's sometimes difficult to have 'enough' functionality after such a short period. In these cases, I recommend common sense and scheduling reviews when you do have more meaningful content. Perhaps scheduling a more internally focused review for the team when you don't.

- Show customer-centric software workflows; try to demonstrate customer problems being solved. The WHY behind the feature, story or sprint goal.
- Connect the Dots…Backward: show how this sprints' work builds on previous work. Show and explain your progress!
- Connect the Dots…Forward: speak to "Coming Attractions" to keep them coming back for more. But then be prepared to deliver on these 'promises'.
- Demand attendance of key stakeholders; if someone has requested or has direct interest in something the team is delivering—they should be there.
- Ask, plead, request, demand, etc…feedback from attendees; then, do something with it in the very next sprint. Demonstrate to your stakeholders that you are listening to them AND taking action.
- Keep your promises, share your challenges, be transparent, be honest, and show enthusiasm.

Helping the Team to Prepare

The Agile and Scrum methods demand working, demonstrable software whenever possible. Be firm in this respect! Sit down with anyone who is orchestrating the meeting and discuss how you can make a good impression; effectively illustrating the work and the business value that the team has provided.

Not every sprint review needs to follow the same *script*. In fact, you may want to vary things to keep your audiences coming back for more. In many ways this is a marketing effort for you and your team, so activate your creative marketing skills, albeit for internal use.

I've seen the following general game plan used _successfully_ in many teams and it may serve to drive your thinking as well. Oh, and one more thing, you're simply helping the team prepare a _high impact_ review here. The overall review is the team's responsibility to prepare, including the Product Owner and Scrum Master, so it should be very much a collaborative effort.

1. **Sprint Goal & Sprint Planning**: As Stephen Covey said[66], you need to "Begin with the End in Mind". Outstanding sprint reviews begin with the goal you converge on in your sprint planning session. And subsequently how you align the work towards it; envisioning working software. And reserving time in your sprint plan for the team to properly prepare for the review.

2. **Discussion:** About half way through the sprint, you might start discussing the review amongst the team in your stand-ups and other venues. This not only gets everyone thinking of the sprint review planning, but it also focuses them on delivering sprint results.

3. **Create a Script:** I usually ask the team to start thinking about the sprint review 'script' that we'll be following in the review. Having a plan for this is imperative. How will you kick-off the review and who will do it? What will the story or feature flow look like? What's the timing – so that everything 'fits' in your time-box? Who will facilitate? I've found that members of the test team enjoy pulling this together and they usually have a more holistic view to the story the sprint goal is trying to tell.

4. **Practice:** Again, you might not always need this and I'm certainly not recommending eight hours of practice for a one hour sprint review. However, you don't want to come unprepared and send _that_ message to your stakeholders either. So, depending on the content, you might want to gather the team and practice your 'script'.

5. **Delivery:** If you've done 1...4, then this is easy. Otherwise...good luck, as you'll need it.

Targeting the Impact, It's Not Only the Features...

I sometimes like to dig a little deeper and demonstrate other things in the review besides just features or stories. I brought up an example of this in the introduction to this chapter that related to *FitNesse tests*[67]. Not only do you want to demonstrate the functionality, but in cases where the value proposition isn't quite clear to the layman stakeholder, you or another

---

[66] This was one of the seven habits in his groundbreaking book: _The 7 Habits of Highly Successful People_.
[67] See Appendix A for more information on FitNesse and Acceptance Test Drivn Development in general.

member of the team should explain the value or the point in terms that are clear and meaningful.

Continued Story

Continuing from that FitNesse point in the chapter introduction –

One team I was coaching was working on a suite of e-Commerce applications. There were parts of the internal logic for one application component that was simply too difficult to test thoroughly. This lack of quality had been frustrating us literally for years! It also surfaced some damaging defects in our customer releases. However, in our case, these bugs could result in lost revenue and/or increased costs to our customers that we'd have to compensate them for – so a very real business impact!

The problem was time and complexity. In order to test all of the permutations of logic, we calculated it would take several hundred thousand test cases that might (a pure guess here folks) take weeks, or even months, to execute; we clearly never had the time for it. What could we do?

First, one of our testers used a testing tool call AllPairs[68] to winnow down the important test cases to a "manageable" set of several hundred tests.

Then the team went about automating all of those via FitNesse tests and fixing the known (now reproducible) bugs in a single sprint. Along the way, they came across three additional critical bugs that our customers hadn't found yet and immediately fixed them.

At the end of the sprint, we had a fully operational set of automated FitNesse tests that thoroughly tested one of our most complex sub-systems. Thus, freeing us to work on more important future stories AND, assuring our customers (and our bank account) wouldn't be affected by this component again.

---

[68] AllPairs is a combinatorial testing tool that attempts to minimize tests run and maximize test coverage by implementing an algorithm for test variable pairing. It's just one approach in a family of approaches to make testing more efficient.

When we demonstrated this in the sprint review, we needed to" set the stage" for the audience, to clarify exactly what we had done. We also needed to explain its significance from a business perspective. Once we did that, everyone applauded the effort. I could even see a serious sparkle (or tear) in the eye of our CEO.

Meeting Dynamics

Here are just a few points that I've found useful creating successful sprint review results and impressions.

Setting the Stage

It's the Product Owner's responsibility to set the stage in the sprint review. They should get up and explain what their goal(s) were for the sprint. They should also to be able to share and express their views as to how the team responded to the challenge.

If the team struggled in the beginning of the sprint with getting focused, but mid-way came together and ultimately delivered towards the goal and 85% of the planned content, then say that. If they exceeded the sprint plan by another five stories, exhausting your stretch items, then say that as well.

Paint a brief, but accurate, assessment of the *team's journey through the Sprint* for the audience.

It's also important to reiterate your thinking behind the sprint goal. What business strategy did you have in mind? What are the critical business and customer drivers? Strongly frame the work that everyone is about to see within a business context.

Not a Demo, Not a Show & Tell; Instead—Valuable and Working Software

This is my experience and background showing through, so bear with me. I've been part of many contrived system demos or a software "show-and-tells". While these were well intentioned events, they often demonstrated software of low quality. For example, our demo scripts were littered with functions and operations to avoid or we had setup the database and data to be simple and correct; just for the demo.

Don't fall into that trap in your review. While you may be delivering stories with limited scope, you should never alter their quality; they should work under all functional conditions. Ensure that your sprint review conditions (systems, people, and execution) amplify quality and, subsequently, _your confidence_.

In addition, take the time to demonstrate your story acceptance criteria with each feature or story. Better that you've automated them, so a simple quick run of the tests with, hopefully, _green_ indications that have all passed. If they haven't already been automated, at least run through them as part of the exposure of each story. I always like the notion of closing the demonstration of each feature with either a firm acceptance (Yes) or give reasons why it deviates from your expectations (No or Maybe).

And between us, the latter should never occur as a surprise within the demo itself!

The Whole Team

The best sprint reviews I've attended are those where the entire team participated in the review; everyone getting the opportunity to show their work. It may create a bit of a hand-off challenge as laptops are exchanged and people move into the _hot seat_, but the effect is powerful in that the entire team is involved in what's going on.

If someone is anxious and neglects pointing out, or demonstrating an important detail, another person on the team comfortably jumps in and covers it for them. Why? Because they're a team and everyone is aware of the overall deliverables. Everyone clearly understands each story's connection to business value and the overall sprint goals.

I strongly recommend a holistic team approach to your reviews, but do it within the context of your team's comfort and ability.

Calling It!

This is an area where I may split with conventional wisdom in the Scrum community. I like having the Product Owner declare victory (or defeat) as an outcome of the sprint review. That is, if the team delivered on the goal, then openly say the sprint was a _Success_.

If they did not deliver sufficient quality or content to meet the goal, then openly admit the sprint _Failed_. While this may be a gray area decision and not a binary or arbitrary decision, I want the decision to be made and stated within the review. Not berating the team, not apologizing, but in simple, transparent terms; honestly and respectfully, telling it like it is.

And again, this should never come as a surprise to the Scrum Master or your team but be more so an extension of the everyday discussions amongst the team; representing their ultimate sprint deliverables.

John Maxwell[69] has a notion he's written about in a book called Failing Forward. In it he reframes the notion of failure being a "bad thing". He tries to reset our lens towards failure being inevitable and that how we handle it and react to it as being the more important point. The notion of failing forward implies that we learn and continuously improve from our failures.

So no hanging of one's head here or guilt or fear; just figure out what went wrong, fix it, and move forward.

Attending the Review—Your Responsibility

As a wrap-up to this chapter, I'd like to share a story that reflects the "attendee responsibility" for each sprint review. Too often, we place all of the pressure on the team and the Product Owner for the review. However, attendees have a professional and organizational responsibility to engage as well.

A Story – Pay Attention in the Sprint Review

It was a hugely exciting evening at iContact. We were pushing a major release to production, which always got our blood pumping. We arrived around 3am on a Saturday morning and began the process of turning an "old version" off and pushing the "new version" in its place. Our target was to have our SaaS application up and running by 8am.

In this release we were pushing a host of internal administrative changes for our customer support team. We'd mostly ignored their needs for the past year in lieu of delivering customer facing features. However, they

---

[69] I could go on quite extensively about this topic/suggestion. It also gets quite a lot of debate in my classes. Before you throw tomatoes at me, please read a blog post I wrote that explains my thoughts in more detail here:
http://www.rgalen.com/blog/2012/5/28/the-agile-project-managerfail-now-as-a-strategy.html

needed some fundamental improvements and we had shifted our development focus to help them.

As we activated the features in our staging and pre-production environments, the customer support folks got a final chance to "try things out" before they went live. After about 30 minutes, the VP of Support suddenly ran back into our release war room and told us to "Stop the Presses". It seemed that some critical administrative functions did not meet their expectations and she wanted to stop and revert the release to the previous version.

I was dumb-founded.

We were using a 4, 2-week sprint release cycle and we'd demonstrated the 'suspect' functionality in every sprint; starting with the first. There were customer support folks in attendance at every sprint review.

In every review we asked for feedback. No, check that, we begged for feedback of any kind – positive, constructive, whining, whatever. That was one of our primary reasons for the demonstration, to see if we were on-track or not in meeting our stakeholders and customers' needs.

Not once did anyone in customer support team say a word; other than clapping and congratulating us on the results. Were they sleeping the entire time? Did they pay attention? Did they care? Well, they had the opportunity to engage and provide us feedback, over the course of 4 sprints (8+ weeks) and they didn't; not until the very last alarming minute.

Long story short: the release happened AND customer support began to fully engage in future sprint reviews.

Adding to the story, Product Owners need to engage the organization in not only attending the sprint reviews, but to ENGAGE in the sprint reviews. It is a responsibility of the entire organization to attend, engage, provide feedback, and think about the implications from their functional point of view.

And everyone needs to remember that catching change EARLY is a critical outcome of the sprint review.

Wrapping Up

❖ By mid-sprint begin assessing your delivery and planning for the sprint review. I've found testers sometimes enjoy the "Master of Ceremony" role in the review, i.e., _conducting_ it.

❖ Leverage a team-based approach for delivering features within the review and have individuals demonstrate their *wares*. This level of accountability and transparency will increase overall done-ness and quality. And do this even if you have remote team members or highly distributed teams.

❖ Always ensure you've explained in layman's terms the business value you've delivered to your sprint review audience. Not only in the invitation agenda, but again in the review itself. In many ways, you're "selling" it to them – so don't be afraid to sell!

❖ Don't be afraid to call your sprint a Success or Failure. Explain why in either case; then inspect, move forward and adapt, as necessary. In fact, you should clearly understand this _before_ the review, so plan your assessment and reactions with your Scrum Master.

Section 4

Product Ownership at Scale

There are four chapters in this section focused towards the dynamics of scaling Scrum and the implications to the Product Owner. This was an area that I was particularly light on in the first edition and I've added quite a bit more content here. It's also an area that surrounds many of the challenges I continue to see in my coaching.

Don't think that scaling in Scrum only applies to organizations with 50+ teams. I've found that organizations with even 2-3 teams need to pay attention to some of the points in this section.

Chapter 16 – Release Planning and Forecasting
If I had a single wish for most Scrum teams it's that they would take release planning more seriously and invest in continuous backlog grooming as a means of preparing for it. So few do it, and few still do it well; and yet it's so fundamentally important.

Chapter 17 – Scrum of Scrums as a Scaling Model
I've spoken to quite a few colleagues who say the Scrum of Scrums simply doesn't work. Personally I've seen it work many times. Scaling is hard. Enterprise agile transformation is hard. Making the model work, and work well, is hard…but, it DOES work.

Chapter 18 – Other Scaling Considerations and Models
Here's a hodgepodge of ideas and extensions to think about when you're scaling your teams. Certainly worth a look; and I think it nicely compliments the previous chapter.

Chapter 19 – Organizational Dynamics of Scaling
Effectively scaling the Product-level organization is central to your agile adoption and Scrum effectiveness. Here we explore ideas surrounding just that – the product side of scaling.

Chapter 16

Release Planning and Forecasting

Great Product Owners are comfortable thinking at different levels within the context of their backlog planning. In fact, they seem to be quite comfortable discussing the nuance of a particular feature or story one minute and then, planning two to three releases in the future, the next. It's this sort of multi-level envisioning that is the most important aspect for this role.

That sounds like a very wide disparity of focus. How do they do it? I believe there are two keys; it's not simply that some are better than others. The first key is leveraging the "just-in-time" nature of the Agile Methodologies. It frees us all for multi-level thinking; in that we don't necessarily have to create all of the details at once. We can envision, implement, and see things unfold rather than predict every detail in advance. Few agile teams fully realize or take advantage of the freedom that this fosters.

I sometimes think of it as _emergent everything_. Agile plans are really roadmaps that we continuously adjust. So, the Product Owner is truly guiding effort _through_ their backlog and not _by_ their backlog.

The second key to success is empowering their entire team to be a part of the envisioning process. They need to inspire them with direction, and then wait for thoughts and ideas to emerge from the team's knowledge gained by making forward progress. It's certainly never a one person show.

This also leads into forecasting as a natural extension to the planning. As the team makes progress, the Product Owner will adjust plans, not only towards business needs, but just as importantly towards the capability and capacity of the team. This sensitivity to the team's velocity allows the Product Owner to continuously improve release _forecasting_ [70] as the team gains valuable experience working together.

---

[70] Steve McConnell introduced the notion of the Cone of Uncertainty for software projects. It reflects the narrowing of estimates and improvement in forecast accuracy as we DO more work on a project and gain knowledge. Steve's context was more waterfall-based in suggesting or recognizing the existence of the cone. In agile projects, I think the cone is even more relevant or even the standard for creating dynamic plans.

Variations in Tempo

One of the first things any agile team needs to establish is its own unique agile tempo. Sure, there is guidance in Scrum that 30 days (4 weeks) is the right length for a sprint. However, that doesn't work for every team. Instead each team should discover their own best tempo with the realization that shorter is better than longer.

There's another decision regarding tempo; that is, how often will you deliver software to your customers? In many in-the-small agile contexts, you hear of teams delivering every sprint. However, in many contexts, this isn't prudent or even feasible. There are a wide variety of factors that influence, what I'll refer to as release tempo, for example:

- Multiple teams working on the same product codebase.
- Working across distributed teams.
- Customer(s) not able or willing to receive releases quite so frequently.
- Size of your product codebase, legacy vs. newer code, and the testing requirements.
- Regulatory or other requirements for completeness in test coverage.
- Production-like hardware availability limits.
- Shared environments and strong cross-team or product dependencies.
- Not having a fully implemented Continuous Integration environment.
- General cost and budget constraints.
- Size of your team and the number of Scrum teams contributing towards the product codebase.

If you can't release every sprint, then you'll need to create additional tempo patterns across your sprints. These patterns usually reflect handling larger-scale work that falls outside the scope of the individual sprint, but is also required to ready the product or project for a release point.

One aspect that often drives this is simply testing. Let's say, for example, you're using Scrum on a legacy codebase that has very little in the way of automated test cases currently available. Instead, it requires execution of a mostly manual test set. You have several millions lines of code and five to seven thousand manual tests. The agile tenants guide us towards testing _everything_ within each sprint. However, here that would essentially derail the entire focus of the sprint. What do you do?

In this case, the answer is to _balance_. Try to test as much as possible within each development sprint. However, you won't be able to perform some types of testing, so you'll accrue some technical testing debt. After a few sprints and prior to a customer release, finish that testing – along with anything else that wasn't done. Surely, this isn't as lean as it should be, and you'll need to be focusing on test automation to increase your testing coverage and speed. However, it is probably still better than the Waterfall equivalent and it does initiate incremental feedback, discovery, and adjustments.

Figure 13, illustrates the three tempos that need to be achieved in each organizations agile instance. First, there is the _development tempo_, where your team is building delivery content. Second, is the _maturation or stabilization tempo_, where they're integrating and solidifying the various work deliverables and, finally, there is your _release tempo_ which is the interval that your customers can expect to see new product functionality.

Clearly, all three can align, or skew, depending on the wide variety of dynamics listed earlier. The most agile view is aligned, but don't fret if you skew a bit. It's quite natural in many contexts.

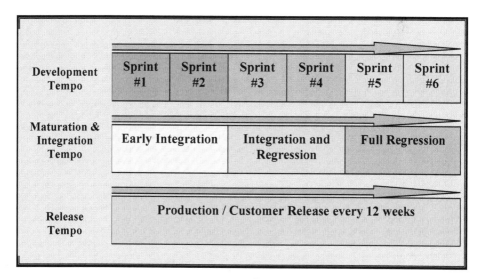

Figure 13, Development-Maturation-Release Tempo Example

The Agile Release Train

Dean Leffingwell, in his *Scaling Software Agility* book, speaks of an Agile Release Train model that helps plan larger scale and legacy-encumbered agile teams. It's the same idea as I presented above, where you change the iteration's focus as you approach planned release points; balancing between content value and production quality readiness.

An important part of the model is the notion of catching the train. Teams work hard on larger-scale features and shoot for specific release intervals in their release planning. They try to complete all work, to their done-ness standards, and catch a specific release target. If they don't get everything done, they don't force out a poor quality release. Instead, they simply catch the next train.

At the time of writing this, *Salesforce.com* [71] is famous for having three seasonal releases a year. Their teams build this into their release planning as features try and catch the appropriate train.

Another part of the agile release train is synchronizing your sprints. It's extremely difficult, if not impossible, to coordinate backlogs across multiple teams if they are all sprinting at different tempos. Instead, you want to align all of your backlogs and sprint planning and review activity so that everything is synchronized. This makes cross-team integration, regression testing, and release coordination so much easier.

Figure 14, depicts graphically an example of a synchronized release train where the teams work for two development sprints. They focus on hardening the work by performing various forms of testing: integration, regression, and performance. Next, they work for three more development sprints, and after that, harden again prior to a customer release point. You can clearly see the various tempos in the example. You should also get a sense for how the backlog might look during these sprints as the type of work focus changes and evolves.

---

[71] Salesforce.com leverages a modified version of Scrum that they have tailored for internal use. Their release model is well documented in their customer interactions and in their external agile presentations. Like all Agile Release Train frameworks, the release tempo permeates nearly all internal and external plans surrounding product release points.

The Agile Release Train
Synchronized

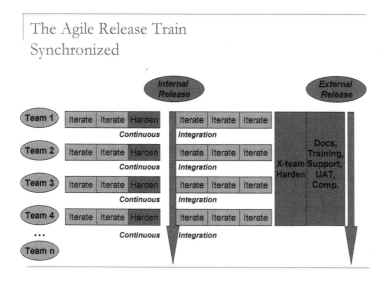

Figure 14, Example of the Agile Release Train

Figure 15, shows an alternative view for a group of teams working in a Software-as-a-Service (SaaS) model. Here, the overall customer release tempo is about every 5-6 weeks. Releases need to be made on a weekend (Saturday) to avoid undue customer impact; therefore, the tempo varies with calendar alignment.

It also is a good example of how software matures by moving forward from a development environment towards a production environment. Often, environment hardware and software costs will increase as you move towards your production environment; which is another reason to shift and/or skew your focus as you target development work towards each release.

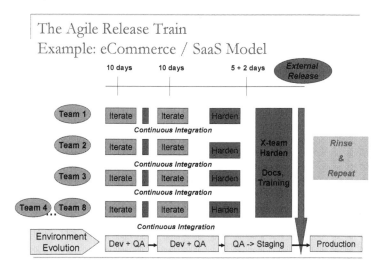

Figure 15, Example of the Agile Release Train in a SaaS Model

The Activities Surrounding Release Planning

Very few recommendations exist for Scrum teams who need to do release planning, so there's quite a bit of confusion as to what to do when; and also how much is enough. I wanted to take some time to create a framework for your thinking around release planning. Much of it ties together other concepts from the book, but I wanted to be a bit more holistic here.

Chartering

First, I want to reiterate that it's part of your agile chartering activities. Often release planning is part of an Iteration #0, even if it only takes you a day or so to plan the next release. I consider it a vision and goal setting activity. It's also part of getting your teams aligned towards a "release-level – body of work".

I like to have a release level Minimal Marketable Feature or Minimal Marketable Product defined before continuing planning. In my experience, stakeholders inevitably want more than the teams are capable of providing within a fix-time interval. Negotiating a *realistic MMP up-front* [72]should be an entry criterion for your release planning.

Look-ahead Grooming

Second, release planning is an _extension_ of your backlog grooming activity. Let's say for example, that your team is quite mature and actively grooms their backlogs. In fact, they typically identify story research spikes ahead of their need and then place their implementation (the research) in earlier sprints.

Suppose you just delivered a release. You've got a 1-week stabilization period post-release deployment. After that, your intention is to spend 1-week planning the next release (and first sprint) and then begin sprinting-forward focused on the next release.

So, essentially you have two weeks to support the production release and get ready for your next release sequence. Let's take a look at your backlog, to see if you're ready. Suppose the following is the state of your product backlog across all 10 of your teams:

- Your velocity is approximately 25 points per team, per sprint.
- Your release train model supports 100 points per team (4, 2-week sprints) OR 1000 total points of capacity for the release.
- You have not done any detailed grooming across your backlogs; because your teams were fully engaged in the previous release.
- Every story is in Epic or large story proportion; each having been examined once by the relevant team.
- All stories are greater than 13 points; indeed, only about 20% are 13 point stories, everything else is 20 points or larger.

---

[72] In the corrective action story later on, the teams literally had 20 customers that were distributed globally. ALL of them had opinions on their needs and priorities for the product release. The project had two Product Owners. A HUGE part of the value in their defining and agreeing on an Minimal Viable Product for the project was narrowing down a unified view that "satisfied" all of those customers.

While it was no easy exercise, relentlessly pursuing it as a goal for "entering" release planning proved quite useful. It placed pressure on the customers to aggregate and agree on a value-based increment.

- You've identified research spike stories along the way, but you didn't have the time to invest in any research.
- In fact, about 10% of your Epics require more research (analysis, prototyping, work) to have a chance to relatively size them.
- You have not thought about any defect reduction investments for the release; or refactoring / infrastructure for that matter.
- You have not thought about vacations, holidays, or any other company-wide or individually significant events that might impact your capacity.

Given the state of your backlog, how far away are your individual teams from planning their next release?

How about readiness across all 10 teams? Meaning creating an integrated release plan with cross-team dependencies, handoffs, integration, and testing accommodated. Could you begin sprinting tomorrow? Should you?

I don't know about you, but I don't think this organization groomed far enough ahead on their backlogs to be _ready_ for release planning. My view is that they require quite a lot of clarity before they can be ready to start sprinting again.

I would recommend that they run an Iteration #0, which is solely focused towards grooming the backlog elements to the point where they can load their teams with well-defined stories for the duration of the release. Remember, this is high-to-medium level planning, so not everything needs to be finely grained, nor understood. It's really a clarity exercise and a commitment exercise for the team to ensure that they have a basic understanding of the work.

BUT

In my coaching, I find more than 50% of the teams enter their next release sequence with less clarity than they should. So, quite often a set of teams, like I described, would charge forth into the release. And they enter the release with a commitment on the table for a release level, body of work. Of course agile teams need to move forward with ambiguity. And of course it's an emergent process.

But, I just don't think entering a release with a _wide gap_ of understanding is prudent for the team or for the business. That's really the intent of release planning. Not to produce a traditional project plan or a false sense of clarity and commitment. But to narrow the unknowns to a point where the team feels they can commit to a feasible body of work that aligns with stakeholder expectations. The emphasis here is on the _commitment_.

A Story of Backlog Grooming Look-ahead

At iContact we had a Release Train similar to Figure 14, except we only had 4 - 2 week development sprints and no mid-release hardening. We found out the hard way that we needed to invest heavily in grooming for the next release during the current release OR ELSE it might take us weeks to make the turn into the next release.

That is if we wanted to be able to commit to a release level body of work that we had confidence in (1) understanding and (2) delivering.

Early on in our agile experience we didn't groom very much. Right after the release, we would begin to sort through stories for our next release. But they were so large and with so many technical unknowns, that we'd often be 'forced' to begin sprinting before we had a thoughtful release plan. It just wasn't possible to wait until we know enough to commit to a release level, "body of work" with some clarity. The business-side just became too impatient – so we would start sprinting.

Usually by the end of the second sprint, we'd groomed enough to understand the whole release workload. Then we checked our capacity alignment with the expectations set when we started. Not once were we able to meet the expectations, which led to this tense, in the middle of a release, negotiation phase; which was just awful.

After a few releases, we re-committed ourselves to grooming a sufficient amount of the backlog during the release; so that we could move immediately into release planning during the transition phase. We even setup _KPI-based_ [73] milestones for sprints 2 and 3, as checkpoints for our team-by team readiness and our overall product release readiness.

---

[73] Key Performance Indicators; defined measures that organizational leadership has in place to measure team results and performance.

Actually, our Chief Product Owner was the inspiration for this pre-work and she made sure the Product Owners and teams were balancing current release work against future release readiness. We reported these out at the Scrum of Scrum meeting; essentially how we were tracking for the "next release"!

I became a firm believer that look-ahead grooming was essential in effective release Minimal Viable Product selection, prioritization, complexity awareness, architecture & design look-ahead, and cross-team dependency preparation. We just needed to remain dedicated to our grooming.

And oh by the way, our leadership team and stakeholders loved the fact that we were able to smoothly envision, plan, and meet our release commitments, within the context of our release train.

Release Planning – Readiness / Entry Criteria

Just as it's incredibly helpful for teams to have story readiness criteria, as we discussed in Chapter 9, it can be helpful to understand what your entry criteria is for release planning. Then your teams can plan the requisite look-ahead work from the previous release and transition periods. To the degree necessary for a smooth release planning period and transition.

Here is a sample set of criteria you might find helpful:

- Based on your team and organizational capacity for the release, minimally that number of stories that need to have been groomed in advance. Preferably the team has seen them multiple times (2-3) and decomposed them a bit.
- All of these stories need to be roughly executable within your sprint time boxes; for example no larger than 8-13 point stories OR T-shirt sizing's with Small, Medium, and Large; with nothing required for the release that is greater than a Large.
- Backlogs need to be effectively targeted toward appropriate teams; based on the release roadmap AND the team skills (see S^3 dynamics later in Chapter 17)
- Research spikes stories have been identified; executed, and resulted in knowledge and a decomposed set of related story(s).

- Cross-team dependencies have been identified at a high-level; major components, activities, feature flow, design, etc.)
- Release criteria has been clearly defined.
- An agreed release train model has been established; preferably you've been using it for previous releases.
- An agreed model for "Hardening or Stabilization" has been established; normally the realm of your Quality Assurance teams.
- Clarity around DevOps (Operational Deployment) dependencies and the work required to "release" the targeted body of work.

Having this information established allows your teams to effectively collaborate and pull together a high-to-medium level release plan for a pre-determined body of work

And as I said, this list helps provide guidance for pre-work during the previous release.

Dependencies are KEY

I can't amplify enough the need to shake out ALL dependencies during pre-planning and release planning activity. That is one of the sole purposes for doing larger-scale release planning with your cross-team members in attendance.

1. Functional dependencies across team(s)
2. Architectural dependencies (from an architecture group and/or individual architects)
3. Design (UX and Software) dependencies
4. Testing dependencies (both on people AND on testing environments and systems)
5. Operations Team (DevOps) dependencies
6. Documentation, Training, Marketing dependencies
7. Other downstream dependencies

For release planning, you don't have to have all of the details sorted out. But I always look for the "dependent parties" to meet around the stories they'll be collaborating on and to commit to being able to deliver features based on a shared understanding and synchronized time or hand-off commitments.

Estimate Granularity

Another one of the keys to effective release planning is NOT decomposing or estimating your stories at fine granularity. I keep emphasizing the phrase: "high-to-medium level" in this section. I'm doing that intentionally to emphasize the size of the stories, and subsequently, the level at which the Product Owner(s) and the team(s) should be planning.

Quite often, because we use the term 'commitment' in our release planning, team's feel a strong need to break everything down into excruciating detail. Essentially researching every unknown or technical challenge; basically, creating a traditional project plan with finely grained clarity.

However, that's not the goal and I don't think it's at all helpful.

It's best to keep your estimates at a level above 5-8 story points or at Large T-shirt sizes. Remember, there will still be ongoing grooming during the release where the teams will continue to break stories down for sprint implementation. So these, larger than you're comfortable with stories, will be broken down further later on. Just not as part of the release planning.

Achieving this balance in sizing is critical to the speed and quality of your release planning. If you don't achieve it, it will take forever to plan.

Blitz Planning & Release Planning

Alistair Cockburn coined the term and the technique Blitz Planning as one of the practices within his Crystal methodology. Crystal is one of the lesser known Agile Methods that emerged from his consulting work at IBM. What's different about Crystal is that it was born out of Enterprise-level clients; so it's particularly interesting and useful in larger-scale agile organizations.

Blitz Planning is a collaborative technique where you basically pull a project team together and you plan a release on a table or wall. Anywhere with sufficient space for lots of cards or post-it notes. Extreme Programming introduced the same notion under the banner of release planning, where you would create iteration swim-lanes visually or a wall or table and moved user story cards around, as the team planned multi-iteration releases.

There were many factors that went into the team-based discussions surrounding work placement, including:

- Team capacity and team skill-sets
- Technical workflow versus. Business workflow
- Dependencies
- Integration and testing activity
- MMP or overall requirements for the release-level, body of work

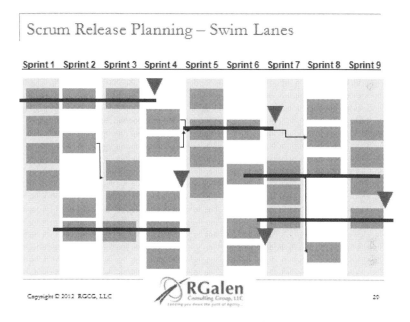

Figure 16, Visual Example of Release Plan Format

That's the essence of Blitz and Release Planning activity, to get the team or teams together and visually plan the work at a moderately high-level of granularity. What you're trying to do is visualize the functional workflow.

It's a collaborative, team-based exercise. You'll want to grab a room for it. Grab a wall and layout your iterative release train model. Then you'll want team(s) to begin laying out their work and their cross-team dependencies visually.

For teams that are new to release planning, I share the analogy that it's simply sprint planning at another level. The same rules apply, layout the work in priority order. Consider swarming around the work. Consider architecture, design, testing, documentation and any other required activity. Add stories as relevant. Move work around based on dependencies.

Figure out how much is "doable" given the constraints of high-quality, high-value, and not burning out your teams. Achieving a visualized plan where all team feel it is a feasible body of work to commit to.

Story-Mapping

Quite often you'll hear the term Story-Mapping in agile and scrum circles when teams are trying to visualize high level product roadmaps and release plans. The strength of release planning is that it lays out a _functional view_ to how the work will unfold.

What is missing is how _customers will actually use_ the product. How will iterations align with usage scenarios and customer workflows? Story-mapping fills in this gap because it organizes sets of stories, features, or themes based on what the customer will be able to do.

There are multiple levels to the story-map:

1. **Backbone**: are the features or themes that the customer will be able to execute with end-to-end workflow
2. **Walking Skeleton**: borrowing the term from Crystal, it's the set of stories that support the backbone.
3. **Sub-Tasks**: are elements of walking skeleton stories; typically these are finely grained supporting stories.
4. **Infrastructure**: this is the component-level or architectural-level work that has to be completed to support the Backbone features.

Visually then, you group sets of features and stories at all four levels that encompass a "usable product increment" from a customer experience (UX) perspective. The "shaded cloud" in Figure 17 illustrates the visual selection of items from the story-map for the very next release.

Typically story-mapping is done before release planning. You would define your Minimal Viable Product. Then construct a story-map to represent what features and workflows will be delivered to the customer. Then those stories would become part of the backlog that would drive release planning; essentially putting the customer (usage) first in your planning.

Figure 17, Story Mapping Example

A Story of Blitz Planning / Release Planning for Corrective Action

I arrived at a coaching client that was midway in the release stream. They essentially had a distributed set of 4 teams along the following lines:

- A distributed User Experience (UX) team with members in North Carolina and the UK.
- 2 front-end development teams in North Carolina; with some members in Brazil.
- 1 back-end services development team; primarily in Singapore; with limited members in North Carolina.
- The teams were 'homed' from North Carolina. There were two Product Owners and Scrum Masters for the 4 teams located in North Carolina.

The UX team was sprinting ahead of the development teams, so they were in Sprint #5 when I arrived. The development teams were in Sprint #4. They were engaged in 12, 2-week sprint release plan that was focused towards updating a worldwide, distributed financial application.

A few days after I arrived, I did a "sanity check" to see how the teams' velocity & progress was lining up with their release commitments.

In a word, they were incredibly misaligned. The teams had delivered at most 5-8% of stakeholder expectations, but were literally 33% of the way through the 12 sprint release plan. So, content was behind. Not only that, they were experiencing nearly daily interruptions from a previous project AND they hadn't technically vetted the committed stories; so technical complexity and risk was surfacing on a weekly basis. To put icing on the cake, they were behind in hiring folks to the "resource plan" that had been used to estimate the release plan.

In a nutshell, they had committed to a body of work without understanding it and then simply started sprinting. The hope was that things would somehow emerge and sort themselves out along the way. That was the "agile way" – wasn't it?

Oh, what to do?

I immediately asked to stop the (insanity) presses. We told leadership that the team had committed to work that they didn't understand and that it was taking much longer than originally thought. We also said that the customers were also changing their minds – leading to requirements churn. Yes, you can change your mind in Scrum, but not in a fixed scope, fixed time model without giving scope relief! Basically, we asked for time.

We began an Iteration #0 or at least what we called an Iteration #0. We first asked the Product Owners to define a "doable" Minimal Marketable Product definition with their distributed set of customers. Initially, there was little agreement amongst the customers and the desire for more than was feasible. It took three days for the Product Owners to come back with a unified and potentially Minimal Marketable Product definition.

Then it was up to the teams. Each team then examined their backlogs relative to the MMP. They worked hard to align their stories to the MMP. In many cases stories were dropped or changed. In many more cases, they were added. ALL stories were re-groomed for clarity and new estimates provided.

In total, the team found about 10-20 of the stories that were too technically challenging for them to estimate or decompose. I quietly thought to myself, how could you have 'committed' to a release with huge, glaring, technical ambiguity holes? But I held my tongue and they ran some fast research spikes for those stories to flesh out the high-level details.

Once we had our overall Minimal Viable Product, Meta-backlog, and Team-centric backlogs, we were ready for Release Planning.

Horizontal – Team-based, sprint planning
First I asked each team to plan their sprint-by-sprint activity for the work they each needed to complete towards the release goal – body of work. I wanted each team to lay out a feasible workflow given their high-to-moderate level understanding of the work.

They needed to commit to the flow as a team and feel good about the quality, work, and map it according to the release plan wall in Figure 18. I also asked them to identify external dependencies, from each team's perspective.

Vertical – Release-based, x-team sprint planning
I then asked all of the teams to "go vertical" on the board. To meet at the board each day and work dependencies, hand-offs, integration testing, cross-team design, literally anything; left to right, one sprint at a time. Identifying dependencies and moving story cards as appropriate until ALL teams felt each sprint was healthy vertically. Then they would move to the next lane/sprint, and the next.

When they all stopped moving to the right and had no more work to place in future lanes / sprint columns, then we were 'Done' with release planning.

Then: Fear, Loathing, Confrontation, Denial, Doubt, and Negotiation

Once the team laid-out all of the work to deliver the Minimal Viable Product, it turned out it would take somewhere between 16-17 total sprints. Given the 4 already completed, that was 12-13 more sprints; or 4-5 more than originally planned AND the MVP didn't contain all of the functionality in the original expectations.

Initially the customers and managers went 'ballistic'.

They threatened to immediately cancel the project. Then to assign it to 'other' teams, who could do the job. They questioned the team's motives, professionalism, and integrity. They were incredibly disappointed.

But then – the thoughtfulness and thoroughness of the plan emerged. We were basing the discussions on a clear MVP and a clear release plan. If the time was too long; then cut something out. So, once the emotional reactions subsided, the Product Owners and the stakeholders negotiated a set of functionality that would have value AND fit within the targeted time-frames.

It's my experience that every release plan results in at least one round-trip of negotiation and scope trade-offs as the REALITY of the work confronts the EXPECTATIONS of your customers and stakeholders. It just seems to be the nature of things. But the good news here is that the negotiation and adjustments are based on team-driven data and plans; not on emotions or perceptions. And the teams are an integral part of the negotiation.

So we settled on a Minimal Viable Product, a defined body of work, and a Release Plan...NOW we were ready to start sprinting again!

Figure 18, Team Release Planning Wall

Story Postscript

I need to apologize to the teams in the above story. It truly wasn't their fault that they'd started too soon and without sufficient team-level understanding. You see, their management had committed them to the project. Their management had analyzed the scope and fit it into a 12 sprint release plan. And their management then composed the teams, handed them their "Product Backlog's", and expected them to immediately start sprinting.

And they did as they were told...

But that didn't mean that what the managers had "cooked up" was (1) feasible, nor did it contain sufficient clarity to (2) connect features with stakeholder needs & expectations.

So, leadership in this example made a clear mistake in not engaging their Scrum teams in early release planning. In this case, it would have saved an awful lot of effort and angst. But in the end and to everyone's credit, the teams pulled this one out and ultimately managed to HIT the release goals.

And the leadership team learned something as well...

Release Planning – Exit Criteria

To wrap up this discussion, it's fair to reiterate the criteria under which a team should be allowed to move into executing a release:

1. Does the project have sufficient charter elements to adequately describe the business expectations? Is an MVP defined?
2. Have the team(s) vetted the product backlog for the work?
3. Do you have well-formed Scrum team(s); that have the requisite skills to do the work?
4. Have the Scrum team(s) laid-out the work in such a way to visualize the workflow for delivery of the MVP definition?
5. Can the team(s) commit to delivering the release?
6. Does the business leadership sign-up to the Minimal Viable Product and derived delivery time-frame?

I usually and literally get the entire group of teams in a room, or as many of them as possible, and look for an overall commitment to the project. I'm not looking for finely grained, we know everything commitment. But, does everyone understand the majority of the work, and the more complex technical challenges? Do they feel comfortable with the overall workflow delivering a well-designed, high-quality product increment?

Do the teams envision themselves being successful? If so, then we go. If not, then we explore what we have to do to raise their confidence?

Refactoring Your Release Plan

Joe Little has written a short (28 page) *guideline*[74] on release planning that aligns nicely with my views. In it Joe establishes the notion or 'refactoring' your release plan at the end of every sprint; reassessing the plan against your team or organizational accomplishments, relative to the release goals. Then making whatever adjustments are necessary to realign things.

I like doing it more on a real-time basis and a visual basis, but the essence of what Joe is saying makes sense to me as well. I'd recommend you read it just to gain a sense for different words and a slightly alternative approach.

---

[74] Here's a link:
http://agileconsortium.pbworks.com/w/file/62413615/Joe%E2%80%99s%20Approach%20to%20Agile%20Release%20Planning%20V1-06.pdf

Wrapping Up

❖ Backlog sprint planning has three basic tempos: Development, Maturation, and Release. You should be factoring all three into your planning.

❖ You need to help your team stay laser-focused on their velocity. Estimates don't really matter that much in Scrum. Rather, sprint-over-sprint output (throughput and velocity) is your key metric for the team's ability to produce value and at what rates.

❖ When forecasting, share your estimates with the team, as well as, all release goal(s) and explain why. Put pressure on them to consistently deliver quality. Also, to deliver on their capacity to each sprint leading to the release. Adjust with them, as it's a two way street towards 'commitment'.

Chapter 17

Scrum of Scrums as a Scaling Model

One of the greatest gaps in the guidance that Scrum creators and community pundits have left open relates to scalability. That is to say, scalability at multiple levels: across products, projects, large-scale and distributed teams, release planning, and product road-maps. There _is_ the nearly infamous Scrum of Scrums that has been defined. But it provides guidance in very high level and general terms, while providing little tactical, day-to-day help in scaling your Scrum instance.

It's basically a hierarchical view towards Scrum dynamics. Ken Schwaber, Mike Cohn, and Jeff Sutherland are some of the Scrum thought leaders that have referenced it but, beyond a simple diagram[75], as seen in Figure 19, and some hand-waving surrounding the concept, Scrum teams are pretty much left on their own when it comes to scaling. I thought it important to at least try and put some additional guidance around the concept based on details from my own implementations of the Scrum of Scrums.

You might ask why does a Product Owner need to understand this; aren't they focused solely on their team and backlog? Well, yes and no. If you're only working in a single team or in a very small organization, then yes, you can probably skip this chapter. But for those of you working as a Product Owner in an at-scale Scrum instance, coordinating your product releases with other Product Owners, then this model can be quite helpful in fostering cross-team collaboration and planning.

---

[75] I got this diagram from Mike Cohn's website. It's been used for years as a graphic that quite simply illustrates the Scrum of Scrums concept. Here you see 3 levels from my perspective. You can find it here - http://www.mountaingoatsoftware.com/scrum/team/

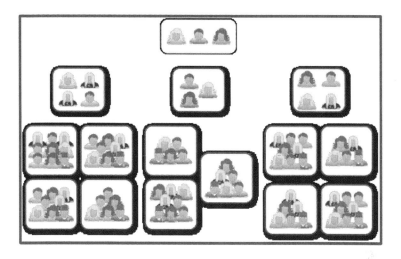

Figure 19, Example of 3-tier Generic Scrum of Scrums [76]structures

Scrum of Scrums implies that you run Scrum at _multiple levels_ in organizations where you have larger scale development. If you have multiple Scrum teams, then the Scrum Masters of those teams meet frequently, using much the same Scrum individual team dynamics to coordinate across their respective teams.

You create a higher level, Meta-product backlog for the Scrum of Scrums that drives work across the teams. From a roles perspective, there will be a Product Owner of Product Owners, call him/her the _Chief Product Owner_ for that backlog. There will also be a Scrum Master of Scrum Masters, call him/her the _Chief Scrum Master_[77]. They will lead periodic stand-meetings

---

[76] This picture is from Mountain Goat Software and Mike Cohn. It's referenced from the Scrum Alliance site in the following article: http://www.scrumalliance.org/articles/46-advice-on-conducting-the-scrum-of-scrums-meeting

[77] To the best of my knowledge, there isn't agreement within the Scrum community as to what to call this second tier and beyond Product Owners and Scrum Masters. I've heard 'Chief' used as well as 'Meta' in some contexts. I'm sure there are others.

In my experience, these roles are often assumed by functional leaders, senior managers, directors or above. Or they are assumed by project managers. Often these roles are the 'glue' between traditional project tracking mechanism and the agile teams.

with, perhaps, slightly different questions and, on the whole, it will essentially be all of Scrum – just *UP a level*.

There will typically not be sprint reviews or retrospectives that represent these aggregated team results. Instead, the individual team reviews need to mention x-team interactions and dependencies and progress towards everyone's overarching release goals.

In my experience, the Scrum of Scrums stand-ups don't necessarily occur on a daily basis. Instead, I often see them occurring once or twice a week. Yes, there is an effort to keep them to the obligatory 15 minutes, but if they run over, that's usually fine. You want to ensure you're surfacing global release state across all of your teams; so take as much time as you need to fully collaborate around your releases.

iContact Scrum of Scrums Tempo Story

At iContact, we would oscillate our Scrum of Scrums quite a bit. It related to our release planning and our release cadence. Around the time we were planning the next release, we would scale back on our Scrum of Scrums; normally to once a week. The meeting was then typically focused on release planning and release readiness discussions.

Once we had a committed release plan and started sprinting, we would move to our normal twice a week cadence. We chose Tuesday and Thursday, late in the day times. Since we were a *SaaS*[78] business, our Scrum of Scrums would focus on our release and on our next targeted "hot fix" package. So, members of our Operations team would normally be in attendance.

As we approached our release target, the Scrum of Scrums attendance would increase, quite often doubling in size with interested parties trying to understand and support the upcoming release. We would also change the frequency of the meeting to a daily cadence somewhere between 1-2 weeks before our release. This made a lot of sense as our release content and preparation decision-making increased dramatically.

---

[78] Software as a Service

We would continue the daily Scrum of Scrums post release until the release stabilized; usually around a week or so. Then we would repeat the process. In essence, the Scrum of Scrums was our "one place" to coordinate our release efforts and our hot fix release stream. It was informative, incredibly well attended, and the best place to understand our progress, impediments, and next step action plans.

Mike Cohn has written *a nice article* [79] on the Scrum Alliance site that explains the Scrum of Scrums dynamic. In it, he changes and extends the basic daily Scrum questions for use in the Scrum of Scrums. Here are the questions he suggests:

1. What has your team done since we last met?
2. What will your team do before we meet again?
3. Is anything slowing your team down or getting in their way?
4. Are you about to put something in another team's way?

These questions certainly speak to broader, cross-team information sharing beyond the first level Scrum. Therefore, you can theoretically scale it upwards for any sized organization. While conceptually this sounds easy; it is, of course, the way you would scale any larger scale software work. The devil, as they say, is in the details of how to implement it within *your* organizational context.

This is where most of the traditional Scrum guidance stops; leaving implementation to each organization. The point is that every organization, beyond the small team agile sweet spot, has some need for Scrum of Scrum dynamics. They need to define, create, and then, refine it for themselves.

From a Product Owner perspective, I've seen multiple levels of defined Scrum of Scrums that you most likely want to participate in. Figure 19, is an example of the layering that I've found to be typical in larger scale Scrum instances.

---

[79] http://www.scrumalliance.org/articles/46-advice-on-conducting-the-scrum-of-scrums-meeting

More often than not, the layers and the focus points are strongly influenced by several key factors:

- The overall size of the Technology or Development organization.
- The number of Enterprise-level products being deployed, as well as, product lines being supported.
- The number of individual Scrum teams contributing (in parallel) to each of the primary product lines.
- The integration requirements across the separate products and product lines. For example: the look and feel, data consistency and sharing, regulatory guidelines, security, and consistent functional compliance testing.
- The existence of a Project Management Office (PMO) function and the negotiated requirements they have for initiating, tracking, and accounting for projects across the enterprise.

It's Not a Formal Organizational Structure!

Don't think of these layers in the same way you might an organizational structure. That would be a mistake. Instead, I like to emphasize their need by illuminating the _conversations_ that naturally happen within larger scale Scrum instances. These conversations occur at _different levels_. For example, Scrum of Scrum (or S^2) conversations usually surround integration and dependency collaboration amongst multiple teams working together on an individual product or project.

Scrum of Scrum of Scrums (or S^3) conversations are at the next higher level of communication. Again, multiple teams are implied, and the conversations surround resource sharing, dependencies, code and component integration and system testing, along with product deployment. Often release planning is a part of the conversation, as is project budgeting and metrics.

Just as an example, I'm basing the structure in Figures 18 - 19 and 21 - 22 on a hypothetical organization where there are three separate products integrated into a _SaaS_[80] framework, with each succinct product having multiple (3-6) Scrum teams contributing application code to each. Given these characteristics, then a Scrum of Scrums framework along these lines _might be_ a useful way to integrate Scrum deliverables and target them towards a customer release train model.

---

[80] Software as a Service

S^1 – The Scrum Team

At this level the conversations surround the individual Scrum team. The team, the Scrum Master and the Product Owner are the primary participants. Sure the Chief Product Owner can and should attend the daily Scrums and other ceremonies, but it's truly about the individual teams.

The focus is on sprint execution surrounding each team's product backlog. This is the place where most of the Scrum guidance is focused, towards the individual team, so I won't belabor the activities here. There is also an important focus on backlog look-ahead via regular grooming meetings.

From a Scrum of Scrums perspective, the team does need to 'care' about externals. For example, dependencies from this team to other teams and impediments they may be causing for other teams. They also need to be aware of the overall release plan and how they fit into it.

But at the end of the day, the team is "heads down" focused on delivering to their commitments.

General Focus of Activities	Product Owner Engagement
1'st level tier, focused towards product development; driving production of high value software components / projects from the individual teams. • **VISUAL: The team Sprint Board** • **VISUAL: The Product Backlog**	Individual Product Owner for each team; defining and driving a specific backlog of work. Demonstrating that work when completed.

Figure 20, Example of S1 level Responsibilities

S^2 – The Scrum of Scrums

At this level the driver is a release or other similar external delivery of software produced from multiple Scrum teams. The primary participants are the Scrum Masters and Product Owners from each team. And of course the Chief Scrum Master facilitates the Scrum of Scrums and the Chief Product Owner is a must-have participant as well.

All of the discussions surround each team's progress in supporting the current release goal and plan. Each *pair of team members* [81] speaks to their support of the goal; are they on track or off relative to their release plans and commitments? Do they have any distinct impediments or dependencies; either in their path or that they anticipate throwing in another team's path?

As the team approaches the release date, an important set of discussions should surround testing, mostly integration and regression, but all testing that is part of the overall release criteria. I would include in this transition talking about operational readiness and deployment activities.

General Focus of Activities	(Chief) and Product Owner Engagement
2'nd level tier, focused towards cross-team collaboration, sprint results integration, and coordination towards the next product release point.	Setup release plan so that the individual teams understand dependencies and expectations surrounding all work (integration, resource sharing, testing, deployment) leading towards the release.
Close to the same dynamics as the Scrum teams; but driven by the overall release plan supporting the roadmap or meta backlog.	Helping teams to manage cross-backlog dependencies and deliverables. Resolving conflicts and issues. Tracking / resolving cross-team impediments.
Often collaborating with cross-team testers during full coverage integration, regression and other forms of *holistic testing.* [82]	
	Connecting team 'state' to the Scrum of Scrums.
• **VISUAL: The Release Plan and the Release Burndown Chart**	Communicating progress to release goal 'outward' across the

---

[81] I think it's a very healthy sign when both the Scrum Master and Product Owner have the same views towards where the team stands. They can both report on "all aspects" of the teams' progress, impediments, challenges, needs, etc. And there is very little "disagreement" between them. It implies that they're working hard in their partnership and in collaborating with their team.

[82] Jeff Patton once described an Information Radiator model that indicated a Happy-Neutral-Sad Face for each component of a product from a testing perspective. Each day the testing team would update the component areas to the real-time state 'face' that represented their feelings. It was a wonderful way to drive cross-team conversation AND keep everyone's eye on the ball for the release.
http://www.stickyminds.com/s.asp?F=S14400_COL_2

• VISUAL: Dependency tracking list , • VISUAL: Impediment tracking list	organization. Ensuring the "release board" is accurate; includes all dependencies.

Figure 21, Example of S2 level Responsibilities

A Release Plan: <u>Central</u> to the Scrum of Scrums

An important distinction to make is that the S^2 usually relates to a planned project release. For example the following is already in place:

- An agile project charter
- A fully vetted and committed Meta-backlog the contains all of the work for a set of teams to complete
- The set of Scrum teams, fully formed to deliver on the work on their backlogs
- A release plan constructed with the team; where they have committed to a realistic "body of work" for a release date

The stand-ups are usually in front of your release plan. Discussions are relative to release goals, plans, dependencies, and assumptions. Progress is tracked across teams, so there is usually a release-level burnup (or burndown) chart that reflects feature level progress for the overall release. Typically the 'units' on this burnup chart are customer facing, committed features and not hours or stories, which are simply too much detail to effectively track at this level.

You're paying attention to cross-team progress, on a sprint by sprint basis, as it relates to your overall release plans versus expectations.

For example, it is not uncommon for the teams to fall behind. Quite often then, the discussion in the Scrum of Scrums focuses on whether other teams can pick up work so that the overall release goal is held. Having a well-planned release map can visually help make these sorts of adjustment decisions and/or guide the team towards scope adjustments.

Transparent & Visual

I personally like the model where the S^2 is a well-publicized event in a consistent location that can accommodate a large group. As I walk through an organization and get the inevitable questions around "How's it going?" I'll invite everyone to attend the Scrum of Scrums as a means of communicating release status information.

I also encourage the attendees to "speak the truth" at the Scrum of Scrums. You always want to be fully transparent with progress so that the entire organization can react to both good and bad news.
Another key is to keep the information on an information radiator in the common place. Figure 22 is an example of a *visual release board* [83] that would be used to track a release. You get an instant visual indication of release state and where challenges might be occurring.

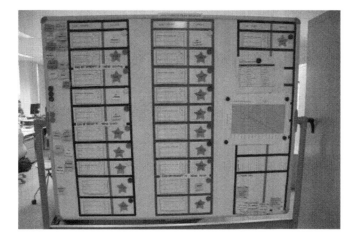

Figure 22, Example of Visual Scrum of Scrums Board

---

[83] There's a wonderful website where I pulled this photo from. It is entitled the Visual Management Blog and provides some wonderful examples of powerful, low-fidelity visual boards for agile teams. Here's a link to a post on S2 visual boards: http://www.xqa.com.ar/visualmanagement/2009/08/scrum-of-scrums-making-it-visual/

George Dinwiddie has a wonderful example of a Multi-Release burndown example of an information radiator here: http://blog.gdinwiddie.com/2012/12/04/multi-release-burnup/

S^3 – Project & Portfolio Planning

Quite a few years ago, I think it was in the 2007-8 timeframe, I was fortunate enough to coach a rather large client instance of Scrum. They had over 100 Scrum teams aligned around three primary product lines. It was virtually identical to the picture in Figure 19, but around 4x the number of teams.

This client had instantiated two additional 'layers' to the Scrum of Scrums model. They called them an S^3 and an S^4, again, abbreviating the repetition of Scrum.

The S^3 was focused beyond the current project. I likened it to be a portfolio management construct but it was more than that. First of all, the S^3 was a place for the Product-side and the Technology-side of the organization to collaborate on future plans. The product folks brought product roadmaps, ideas, and fairly aggressive forecasts to the table. The technology folks brought their team's skill sets, capacity, and capabilities to the table. They would also bring future hiring plans and budgets into play.

Quite often, cross-cutting concerns were a primary part of these discussions, for example, exploring how to effectively integrate UX, Enterprise Architecture, Shared QA, and Shared Deployment or DevOps within the Scrum teams.

Then, at a high level, the two groups would forecast out roadmaps and team plans (team composition, backlogs, team-to-product mappings, identity, skill-set alignment, architecture alignment, UX alignment, etc.) that aligned organizational teams towards product execution.

S^3 Logistics

The S^3 rarely meets on a regular basis. Instead, a meeting is normally called only when needed. For example, if you are halfway through the current release and getting ready to groom the backlog for a high-level plan for the next release, you might want to have an S^3 level meeting to discuss preparation for planning, staging, and kicking off work.

Another focus of the S^3 in this case might be instantiating the project in your phase-gate model [84] in gaining organizational leadership approval. Your S^3

---

[84] These models are connected to the phases of Waterfall process. For example, you might have an "approval phase or gate" between the requirements complete phases

team would then meet as appropriate and pull together the charter, business cases, and high-level estimates as appropriate for approvals.

Sometimes you don't need a meeting at all. I remember at iContact we would sometimes shift people from team to team based on our growth and attrition. In these cases, we would send out an email with the proposed changes to our S^3 list and wait a few days for feedback. Then, we'd simply make adjustments as needed; then make the change.

We tried very hard to collaborate between Technology and Product on all aspects related to our teams executing our release backlogs. You'll see more on this in the next chapter under the Triad discussion.

To the question of who engages with the S^3, the short answer is "it depends". Clearly this is a "management-level" meeting. So your product and technical leadership teams should be a part of this. I usually do not include the Scrum Masters and Product Owners directly in the discussions unless we have some point questions for them or want to get their advice on a nuanced change or adjustment.

Clearly the first folks who are apprised of S^3-level discussions, decisions and straw-man plans are the relevant Scrum Masters and Product Owners. In fact, they usually are the ones tasked to guide the changes within the teams.

General Focus of Activities	Chief Product Owner Engagement
3'rd level tier, intended to focus on staffing, resource sharing, product portfolio management, ROI, etc. from the various projects.	Business case development, phase-gate control for beginning projects.
Can also drive cross product line consistency, for example, look and feel, quality levels, and regulatory and security requirements.	Portfolio planning leading towards effective people & resource utilization and balancing.
Often drives budgeting and overall product portfolio planning across a particular larger scale or enterprise-	Defining overall product/project consistency goals: usability, quality, security, regulatory / certification, etc. Running planned Alpha/Beta

and software construction phase. Usually specific artifacts are defined and a meeting is held to review your readiness to "pass the gate".

level product(s) or product family(s).	programs. Deployment strategies.
• VISUAL: Usually a longer term road-map that spans multiple products (Portfolio) • VISUAL: Usually some sort of spreadsheet capturing teams, skills, capacities, and focus	Overall committed release plans and external coordination within cross-functional teams. External partner and 3'rd party integration.

Figure 23, Example of S3 level Responsibilities

S^4 – Agile Steering

The fourth level of the Scrum of Scrums model that I was exposed to at my client and have adopted in a wide variety of my own coaching experience, has very little to do with projects. The S^4 is effectively all about steering your agile methods. It focuses on defining and adhering to your practices; having baseline guidelines for your agile methods, your roles, and your tactics. It also revolves around your agile capabilities and establishing the training and coaching your teams might need to improve their execution performance.

There are many ways to steer agile adoption and transformation. So the S^4, while it tries to adhere to basic Scrum practices and behaviors, can take on three common flavors. I'll explore the Scrum variant next and the other two in the next chapter.

S^4 as a Scrum Team

In this instance, the S^4 operates as a Scrum team. You find a Scrum Master and form a team that will be focused on guiding organizational agile adoption and transformation. Clearly the team will need a Product Owner and a Product Backlog. Quite often, the members of senior leadership who are championing the adoption will serve in this role.

Next the team brainstorms the backlog of all activities required to instantiate, grow, and evolve Scrum. Then it's simply a matter of sprinting towards accomplishing these items. Often all of the ceremonies are applied; with the sprint review and retrospective being particularly useful in making the adoption progress and plans transparent across the organization.

Since agile adoption can be complex, often the backlog is sliced into initiatives, which is synonymous with releases. Goals are established so everyone has something to "shoot for". And of course, as in any project, there are risks, dependencies, and adjustments that are required.

I've often seen a quarterly tempo used for work at an S^4 level. This usually aligns nicely with typical organizational transformations and executive reporting. It also allows some time to make significant progress between releases. There can also be the need for S^2 like meetings for making tactical progress and cross-team impediments more visible.

General Focus of Activities	Chief Product Owner Engagement
4'th level tier, in my experience tending to focus towards Scrum and Agile adoption strategies and training across the entire organization.	Chief Product Owner is fully engaged here at a leadership level focusing on Enterprise-level goal setting, defining long term agile evolutionary road-maps.
Leading in defining 'standards' or guard rails for cross-team Scrum utilization.	Participating in or delegating individuals to help 'steer' agile adoption
Perhaps including focus groups for Scrum Masters and Product Owners.	Effective staffing and training strategies of Product Owners are also defined here.

Figure 24, Example of S4 Level Responsibilities

A Final "Scrum of Scrums" Story

A short time ago, I had a development organization in St. Petersburg, Russia that was split up in two scrum teams to work on a couple of products. These products were very different in functionality, but shared a common UI, data storage, and communication layer. The teams shared a Test manager, a Research and Development manager / Scrum Master, a Business Analyst, and the Product Owner. The majority of the other team members were assigned to one of the two teams.

A few of them were assigned to a team on a release basis (4 sprints) or a sprint basis depending on the technology affected by the release or the focus of the sprint. For example, sprint #4 was typically focused on getting the product ready for release to one (or multiple) customer(s). This sprint, therefore, always had more testers than other sprints.

We would skew the releases and sprints so that we would have the maximum amount of time between sprint end/beginning and the same for the releases. This way, we could shift people for specific sprints with minimal impact on the other project. We were also able to focus better on the needs of a specific team. The Product Owner, the Scrum Master, and the business analyst would participate in product demos, sprint reviews, and sprint planning for both products.

We had daily stand- up meetings where the entire team would participate, as well as, weekly meetings to discuss the integration of technology and plans with the Scrum Master, test manager, and architects. In this meeting, we would make decisions regarding higher level architectural or strategic directions. In general, these were things that would either not affect the team in the next couple of sprints, or, they would affect both teams equally.

We (the Product Owner, Scrum Master, and sometimes the business analyst or architect) additionally had regular meetings where we would discuss process optimizations, technology needs, and/or lessons learned. These meetings were held on a regular basis, but without a scheduled time. Most meetings were scheduled whenever there was a need – usually, every 2-4 weeks. Follow up meetings were planned to work out details and tracking changes to ensure that all changes were a step forward, rather than a step backward.

Furthermore, we had quarterly planning meetings with representatives of Sales and Marketing, as well as the executive team to track our progress, refine plans and to adapt to changed business needs. This was the time to get a formal "thumbs up" stating that we were still on the right track (or, if not, to change accordingly).

Having thought about this more, I realize I was having four levels of Scrum of Scrums :-). It just never felt as structured or rigid as it seemed on paper...

—Michael Faisst

I like Michael's story because it emphasizes the collaborative looseness and application of common sense that needs to be an integral part of your Scrum of Scrums definition. It also helps illustrate the different conversations that are essential for effective collaboration.

Wrapping Up

Is the Scrum of Scrums always the answer for Agile & Scrum scaling? I don't think so. But it can be effective in many contexts.

I remember talking to a fellow coach from a large company that was a competitor of ours at iContact. One of the reasons that they chose to move to Kanban was that their Scrum of Scrums were basically dysfunctional. It was not helping them with cross-team collaboration nor effectively integrating to their Operations team for *product deployment*[85].

As we discussed the dynamics of what went wrong, it became clear to me that the Scrum of Scrums hadn't failed. It was his organizations culture and their implementation of S^2 activities and behaviors surrounding it that were flawed.

For example, key contributors didn't bother showing up at the Scrum of Scrums. And they didn't lead it with holistic release planning. There were other problems, but in general it wasn't an S^2 problem, it was a planning, collaboration, and commitment problem. We realized together that their move to Kanban wouldn't fix these problems, but it might shed a different light or view to them; so the organization could improve.

Point being – implementing an effective Scrum of Scrums hierarchy can be incredibly hard. However, it can also be the difference maker for project results at scale.

---

[85] The product in this case was a SaaS

Chapter 18

Other Scaling Considerations and Models

It turns out that the Scrum of Scrums is not a panacea for scaling, nor does it factor in all of the considerations that many organizations need for successful scaling. I wanted to explore a couple of 'extensions' to the last chapter that are important in your thinking about agile scaling from the perspective of the Product Owner.

I hope some of the concepts will prove valuable as you partner in your organizations adoption and scaling of agility. All of these ideas are complimentary to the Scrum of Scrums model, so I don't mean to suggest 'replacements' for it. I'm actually quite fond of the model and have made/seen it work in a wide variety of enterprise environments.

First, I want to explore a few models that will help with standards and guidelines at scale.

Alternatives to the S^4

In the last chapter I introduced the notion of an S^4 for agile adoption and transformation steering. It is certainly one way to do that. There are two other complimentary methods that are also popular for agile steering: the Center of Excellence (CoE) and the Community of Practice (CoP) models. Both have worked well to help guide agile adoption and we'll explore them briefly next.

Establishing a Community of Practice (CoP)

One model is to establish a Community of Practice. This is usually a very 'soft' approach in its guidance. I've seen it often implemented as a set of agile guidelines, references, and examples on a wiki page with a loose organizational group that is aligned to:

1. Caring and feeding of the references and examples, and
2. Meeting occasionally to discuss how the teams are leveraging the repository and future needs.

The CoP is intended to grow more organically from within the teams and doesn't really intrude on their day-to-day activities. Consider it more of a 'reference' for how to operate Scrum organizationally.

Quite often leadership of the CoP comes from within the teams, particularly from within the core of Scrum Masters, Product Owners, and Scrum of Scrum(s) groups.

Establishing a Center of Excellence (CoE)

Finally, the Center of Excellence model is a more prescriptive version of the CoP. Here practices are considered to be mostly mandatory and there are normally mechanisms put in place to measure adherence. For example, your team, project, and organizational done-ness criteria would be established as CoE-level norms and adhered to across teams and projects.

More formal agile coaching is often part of the CoE, so there might be a team of coaches that not only lead the direction of the CoE, but also collaborate with the teams to cross-train and reinforce practices. They might even perform "practice assessments" of teams in order to drive maturity and consistency.

Keep in mind that none of these models are intended to operate as a traditional CoE, which dictates consistent practices, in the smallest of detail, across ALL teams. That's simply counter-productive to developing high performance, self-directed teams.

Consistency at a Product Owner Level

In all of these cases, the product organization should be an active partner in the agile adoption and transformation landscape. You'll want to engage and contribute as required; particularly when it comes to the methods, roles, processes, and artifacts you'll be using for Scrum Product Ownership.

The Chief Product Owner is typically thinking in terms of many groups and products, so aligning some standards across 'product' makes a great deal of sense.

N-Levels of Agile Planning

Another typical scaling challenge is cross-team and cross-product planning. Do you remember in Chapter 3 where I mentioned that the Product Owner is "part Project Manager"? Well, I didn't misspeak in that reference. I believe that the Product Backlog is the new planning vehicle in agile teams. It is the one agile artifact that revolves around workflow, dependencies, risks, milestones, formal testing cycles, and iterative delivery. It's the one size fits all "project plan" for agile teams.

A common analogy for agile planning is that of an onion. There are many references to the *Agile Planning Onion*[86]. I have a tabular representation of the onion in Figure 25. In it, there are 5-6 layers that are commonly referred to. I like to group them based on frequency. For example, the continuous, daily and iteration levels are essentially part of basic agile execution. I consider it the heartbeat that we observe and measure in our construction efforts.

The release level is unique. It's the 'glue' between iterative execution and the higher level strategic and portfolio planning functions that are required in the agile enterprise. As we discussed in Chapter 16, release planning is a fundamentally important part of composing higher-level business goals into tangible release packages for customer consumption.

Strategy and portfolio management are at the highest layers. These are typically the domain of your executive team, product organization, creative envisioning design, and software architecture and design teams. These ideas need to be ordered, validated and sufficiently explored so that they can be release planned by their respective team(s). While your agile teams might get "pulled into" some of this collaboration, typically this is a leadership-led activity.

---

[86] I'll be using the VersionOne video reference for the book, but you can find many others. Here's the reference - http://www.youtube.com/watch?v=cmqmNWWQ5-4 Some define it as 5 levels and drop the continuous planning part.

Others have suggested to extend it, for example Kelly Waters has suggested here - http://www.allaboutagile.com/the-agile-planning-onion-is-wrong/ that Culture is missing above Strategy. Now that I think about it, I happen to agree with Kelly; although culture isn't necessarily a clear aspect of "planning".

I would also add that much of this activity and conversations would occur at an S^3 level, as described in the last chapter.

Onion Level	Activities, Drivers, Focus Points	Frequency
1. Strategy	Vision, Ideation, Creative, Customer	Periodically, Continuously
2. Portfolio	Program, Forecasts, Valuation, PMO, Governance	Quarterly, Continuously
3. Release	Project, Charter, Release Train, Hardening, Feature Burnup	Release Cadence
4. Iteration	Sprint, Cadence, S-Curve, Risk, Dependencies, Story/Task Burndown	Sprintly
5. Daily	Scrum, Stand-up, Transparency,	Daily
6. Continuous	Integration, Deployment, Stop-the-Line	Daily

Figure 25, Tabular view of the Agile Planning Onion

As an engaged Product Owner, it's important to understand the overall planning activities within your agile teams. Sure, you may not fully participate in all of these layers, but you do want someone in your organization to be handling each of these in succession. Otherwise, you'll find that you're planning, execution and delivery, disconnected from your higher level expectations.

Mike Cottmeyer has a wonderful model [87] that he shares regarding 3-levels of orchestration when it comes to funneling work from the top of the organization (leadership) down to the bottom (teams). In fact, he alludes to different agile methods being used to orchestrate the flow. Rally Software has recently added the same sort of notion to portfolio management

---

[87] Mike has his own Agile Consulting firm called LeadingAgile. Here's a link to their general resource page: http://www.leadingagile.com/agile-resources/ and here's a link to a presentation about Scaled Agile Transformation Patterns: http://www.slideshare.net/mcottmeyer/exploring-agile-transformation-and-scaling-patterns

capabilities in their Enterprise ALM^{88} product. Both of the models speak to Kanban orchestrating the validation flow of enterprise level project work that is intended for multiple teams.

Kanban's pull model, based on visual workflow dynamics, is ideal for senior leadership and other core functions (architecture, analysis, design, business case development, portfolio costing, etc.) to filter into "digestible chunks" for the organizations release processes. It also implies a pre-preparation or readiness model, where work items (Epics) are pre-worked to whatever degree is required to get them into a stream of work that teams can analyze, plan, and execute for delivery in release(s).

Onion Level	Story Granularity and Activities	Method of Execution
1. Strategy	Portfolio-level stories (EPICS); Ideation, High-level product roadmaps, technology roadmaps	Kanban
2. Portfolio	Project-level stories; (FEATURES or THEMES) Business case; high-level sizing; valuation, design look-ahead	Kanban
3. Release	Features and MMF's; Packaging themes into a release; Mid-level sizing	Scrum, Blitz Planning
4. Iteration	Executable stories; they fit within sprint boundaries	Scrum
5. Daily	Scrum, Stand-up, Transparency,	Scrum
6. Continuous	Integration, Deployment, Stop-the-Line	Scrum & XP practices

Figure 26, Planning Onion Mapping to Levels & Management Methods

Figure 26 and Figure 27, illustrate the 3-phase model that is quite useful in pulling work into teams from Portfolio through Project through Release & Execution levels within larger-scale Enterprise agile adoptions.

---

[88] Agile Lifecycle Management. Typically this acronym is used for agile tools that try to encompass the entire agile SDLC, from portfolio planning to deployment or delivery.

The key is for the upper level structures to have just enough work thoughtfully prepared for execution so that there is an even workflow into the releases and teams. That encompasses two ends of the pipeline, the inflow pipe for pre-work and the outflow pipe for deploying to customers.

There might even be the case where there is some queuing going on at both ends as the organization is dealing with more traditional, Waterfall preparation and deployment capabilities. In some cases, this is even advantageous, as an agile migration phasing strategy as the organization ramps-up to a leaner, more continuous flow model.

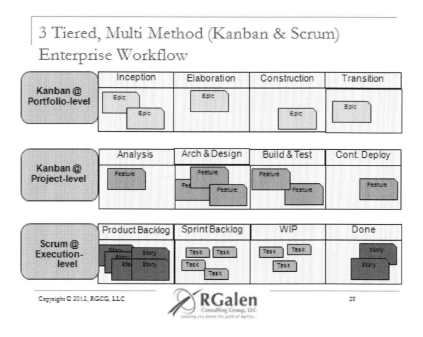

Figure 27, 3 Tiered, Multi Method (Kanban & Scrum) Enterprise Workflow

Other Scaling Frameworks

There are two other frameworks that are becoming popular in the agile community that I thought I would just touch on.

Scaled Agile Framework (SAFe)

Dean Leffingwell has introduced his SAFe or *Scaled Agile Framework* [89] within the last year or two. He's recently introduced a variety of certification levels surrounding it as well.

SAFe is primarily targeted towards the agile enterprise. Dean's historical experience is in Rational Unified Process (RUP), so you'll see similarities between it and SAFe. Dean has long been a partner of Rally Software and you see connections between the framework and Rally's tooling.

SAFe is a 3-tiered model, much like we've been discussing. Probably the key difference is the amount of guidance that is provided amongst practices and approaches for implementing the framework; very reminiscent of RUP level guidance…and growing. SAFe also supports the pre-development sprint (Iteration #0) and post-development sprint (Hardening or Stabilization) sprint models that we discussed earlier in the book.

Disciplined Agile Delivery

Scott Ambler has introduced a book and a methodology entitled *Disciplined Agile Delivery* [90] or (DAD). Scott has been augmenting the agile methods for years with ideas surrounding architecture, design, and modeling. His background has long been in IBM consulting and methods and he has a relatively strong RUP background as well. So much of his advice surrounds bridging these classic practices towards agile development.

Instead of being a 3-tiered model, DAD is essentially an iterative extension to Scrum with some strong recommendations for architecture, design & modeling, and deployment practices. It also defines a very broad set of team-based roles. There are three primary 'phases' to DAD projects:

---

[89] You can research more on SAFe here: http://scaledagileframework.com/ The framework is essentially in the open source community, although there's quite a bit of focus on 'certifications' at a variety of levels.

[90] More on DAD can be found here: http://disciplinedagiledelivery.com/ Also keep in mind that the methods are described in Scott's book by the same name.

Inception, Construction, and Transition; which again, are reminiscent of RUP style projects.

Both SAFe and DAD are interesting variants for agile wrappers or frameworks for at-scale implementations. The danger I suppose, and it is a real one, is that organizations will focus on implementing the frameworks and not go through the "situational hard work" to find out what works for them. Another danger is thinking that the framework is a silver bullet in achieving "agile mindsets" within their teams and organizations.

That was and still is one of Scrum's strengths. While it is billed as a 'framework' as well, it is a minimalist framework, which leads to organizations being left on their own a bit to tailor and *think about* agility.

Architectural & U/X Coordination

Another important part of the Scrum of Scrum's discussion is technical and cross-team coordination. I think great Product Owners push their backlogs, and subsequently their teams, towards the relentless pursuit of zero dependencies.

The complimentary force to this is that most developers push towards greater dependencies. They're more comfortable with larger scale features developed "in-the-large", that require greater cohesion. I get the sense this comes from our traditional training and experience in how to build software architectures. In your role, you want to constantly challenge teams to break things down. But, more important than that, to try and break things down into component parts that have few and extremely loose dependencies.

There's a wonderful *blog entry* [91] by Mike Cottmeyer that speaks to dependencies as being one of the critical challenges in enterprise level agile scaling. In a nutshell, he alludes to successful agile scalability being directly tied to the organization's ability to create products, features, stories, components, tasks, etc. that are decoupled from one another. In other words, minimization of dependencies; thus, enabling each small Scrum team to be able to deliver value on their own right and not encumbered by the work of other teams.

When you do have dependencies, then the Scrum of Scrums structure is a good way to make them visible across various teams that are trying to

---

[91] http://blog.versionone.net/blog/2008/12/the-secret-to-organizational-agility.html

manage them. Next, we'll explore a few strategies for collaborating when you do have dependencies.

Visiting Pigs

One practical approach I've seen work for handling cross-team dependencies being driven from the Scrum of Scrums, is to foster dependency team membership by including team members as *visiting Pigs* in other Scrum teams. When two teams have a clear dependency, then one team sends a 'visitor' to the other team's sprint planning and daily stand-up meetings to ensure representation and to maintain dependency continuity.

Quite often, these visitors have an architectural view, or slant, within the team – so they're more or less, ensuring that work meets higher level architectural goals and/or standards. Nonetheless, this is an effective way to make cross-team dependencies visible so that both teams can properly handle them.

Other Approaches

We discussed an important dependency management point back in Chapter 9 under Readiness Criteria. One powerful way to connect dependencies is to not allow dependent-driven stories to enter any team *until* all of the dependencies have been *glued together* across their respective dependent team(s). Regardless of how many teams are involved. And this implies that all of the teams commit to meeting their parts of the dependencies.

In general, you want to push dependency management down to the lowest level for 'management'. While you want to make them visible on your S^2 and S^3 level information radiators and tracking boards, that's doesn't get ownership low enough. It just shows you the dependencies.

You'll want your Scrum Masters to be aware of the dependencies and then encourage team members to "take ownership" of gluing them together. Next I'll share a story that has another suggested approach for handling dependencies.

Story – Another Approach for Integrating Architecture

At ChannelAdvisor, we had approximately 8-10 Scrum teams running in parallel on three separate product lines of a SaaS eCommerce product offering. Architectural coordination was one of the things we struggled with most.

Initially, we had separate architectural groups that were tasked with providing architectural guidance across all of the teams. We noticed, however, that since the architects didn't operate within a working Scrum team, their ideas had a "throw it over the wall" flavor to them, which didn't sit well with the teams. In spite of this, they did need time to consider system level architectural designs independent of all other activities.

The teams eventually hit on a compromise that seemed to work quite well.

The architects (UI / Usability, Middleware and Database) would attend all of the sprint planning sessions across our (8-10) teams; looking for opportunities where they were needed or could engage in the sprint work. They would sign-up for work on a team at a 50% utilization level based on their perceptions of cross-team dependencies, needs, and opportunity.

This arrangement provided some real 'glue' between our teams at the discrete technology level that we didn't have before implementing it. Because it was self-directed and adaptive to what our overall Meta Product Backlog required, the results were better than when we were more prescriptive in assigning our architects to teams.

The Triad – Partnership Between Product, Quality, and Development

Ken Pugh has written about *The Triad* [92] from the perspective of ATDD or Acceptance Test-Driven Development; constructing executable requirements via tools such as Cucumber. It's an extension from the user story acceptance tests that are a part of each and every story. See Appendix A for more information.

The Triad in this case is the partnership between the Product Owner, developer(s), and tester(s) on Scrum teams as they execute and deliver stories. It's indicative of the *swarming* [93] that can be incredibly effective in driving agile work and minimizing hand-offs and delays.

---

[92] Ken Pugh wrote: *Lean-Agile Acceptance Test-Driven Development: Better Software Through Collaboration* in 2011. In it, he references the Triad as a metaphor for effective agile collaboration.

[93] Swarming simply implies that team members work together on getting something done rather than working serially based on their skill-set and then handing off work

Leveraging this metaphor beyond the team level, I believe there is a *Triad in play*[94] in effective Enterprise-level agile adoption. Instead of the traditional silos that exist organizationally; via traditional organization structures, there needs to be more collaboration between these three functions. And I think it drives through the product organization; i.e., the product organization takes the 'lead' when it comes to planning and releasing software.

This connects to the S^3 discussions in the last chapter. But I didn't amplify the product leadership part of the equation. Perhaps this story will help:

Story on Triad Partnership and Product Leadership

When I was a Director of Development in a traditional Waterfall organization, I did the entire project planning for my development projects. The product organization would throw the roadmaps "over the wall" to my teams for execution. I would do the requirements analysis, project plans, negotiate with the product folks, and then commit to a plan.

In the end, I would throw the software "over the wall" to the quality group for testing & requirement verification. Then we would both throw it back over the wall to product organization for customer delivery.

While we were ostensibly an "organizational team", our first loyalty was to our functional silo. But this posture fundamentally changes as you move towards an agile organizational transformation.

For example, during my tenure at iContact I found myself vetting our technology organizational development plans earlier and more collaboratively with the Chief Product Owner and the product team. For example, vetting team structures with them, aligning hiring plans with the roadmaps, vetting our skill set strengths & weaknesses and overall team development plans.

---

to each other. Typically teams 'swarm' around getting a User Story completed as soon as possible within a sprint.

[94] I've written a blog post that explores this in a bit more detail. It also has a nice story that supports the notion at multiple organizational levels. You can read it here: http://www.rgalen.com/blog/2012/5/29/the-agile-project-managerthe-triad-at-the-heart-of-agile-col.html

This even extended to how we aligned teams towards our products. We just didn't throw people into teams, throw backlogs together, and then glue them together. No, it was much more thoughtful than that. This is the basic ordering of our thought processes over time:

1. It started with the product roadmap. Understanding what we were trying to accomplish strategically as a business. Looking at it from a technology perspective and trying to contribute (early) to the plans from our perspective.

2. Next we would look at the overall development and testing organizations, trying to determine numbers, skill-sets, and groupings to best connect teams and skills to product areas in the roadmap. All with an eye to efficient throughput of features.

3. Part of the above was considering Scrum Master and Product Owner 'pairs' for each team. Also, the nature (types of work) that each backlog would feed each team. Were we skill aligned? Consider this close to *Feature Team and/or Component Team* [95]alignment; although we didn't directly leverage those notions.

4. We tried hard to give each team an identity or ownership of a complete area of the project or product. Ownership of maintenance, bugs, new development, support, dependencies, architecture, etc. We felt it important for each team to have a strong sense of ownership, which then aligned towards accountability.

5. We would also consider load balancing; were we balanced to product priorities across the roadmap as much as possible given our team size and capabilities? In these cases, we might create shared responsibilities (backlogs, architecture, etc.) across multiple teams.

---

[95] There are two methods that many agile organizations use to map teams to the development areas within the product. One is a Feature Team model, where teams are put together to work on quite large-scale aspects (Epics / Features) of a given product. The other model is a Component Team model, where the teams are aligned towards more long lived component areas within a product.

Advantages of these models are team-cohesion, knowledge continuity, and ownership of product areas.

In my traditional team experiences, we would never have partnered this way. But we did here within our agile contexts and it worked beautifully.

For those wondering if we lost ourselves in the partnership, I'd say no. We didn't always ask for permission. And the product team valued our technical leadership capabilities and trusted our judgment. But we were much more collaborative and transparent than I ever was traditionally.

Wrapping Up

❖ The planning onion is an important metaphor to remember and implement a variety of levels in your agile planning. Sure, you can leverage Scrum vs. Kanban, but the important part is effectively planning the flow of valuable work through your agile teams.

❖ Too many agile transformations are reluctant to have strong standards of execution. I think this is a mistake; especially for Shu-level teams. Don't be afraid to setup a CoP or CoE model with some constraints on how your teams operate.

❖ Mike Cottmeyer has written and presented about (dependencies) and (cross-team communication) being two of the biggest problems in agile at scale. While you won't 100% solve this with any of the approaches, I fundamentally believe planning for these challenges and making decisions and issues visible and transparent is the way forward.

❖ Esther Derby has a nice slide deck that is entitled: Agile Teams at Scale: Beyond Scrum of Scrums. Its available here: http://www.slideshare.net/estherderby/agile-teams-at-scale-beyond-scrum-of-scrums In it she focuses on some of the social dynamics that are required in cross-team interaction at-scale. You might find it interesting.

Chapter 19

Organizational Dynamics of Scaling

Agility, when first introduced in the guise of Scrum and Extreme Programming, was very much a small context play with small co-located teams of less than ten members. They worked directly with customers or their advocates and utilized heavy face-to-face collaboration. In addition, they displayed a strong focus on the in-the-small, quality-centric, development practices.

They also developed relatively small applications, typically not at the Enterprise-level, or for real-time safety critical applications, or large-scale and regulated applications; that just wasn't the sweet spot for the methods at the time. However, web applications were definitely an area of strength because of their UI-centric nature where the customer really did need to continuously engage in their evolution.

Since agile methods were not a prescriptive process, but a learned and adaptive one, there was (and is) very little in the way of guidance. You really had to gather some information by initial reading or training, then gain your real _agile chops_ by raw experience. Again, that works well in small teams.

However, as agility begins to become a more mainstream methodology, it is encountering more situations that are outside of its core context or sweet spot. While the methods can and do adapt quite well, it takes additional work, energy, and effort to do so successfully.

It also requires a person to adapt the methods beyond their simple natures and, potentially, _stretch_ them towards the more traditional approaches they're intended to replace. Or, at the very least, learn to interface with those more traditional approaches.

Therefore, this chapter is for the great Product Owner who is working in contexts outside the scope of _small agility_. I'll try to touch on specific areas where you might need to make adjustments in order to increase your effectiveness.

Scaling the Product Owner Organization

If operating as a Product Owner in a team is broad and challenging, and it is, what does it feel like when you have multiple teams contributing software towards the same product or application? Imagine that there are eight independent product backlogs and eight independent Product Owners driving towards the same product goal, but in an uncoordinated fashion.

Sounds like chaos to me! How about you?

To effectively integrate the team's work, there needs to be a common or shared backlog that is a super-set of all eight teams' work. It actually speaks to features, but also to relationships, dependencies, and boundaries for the entire project. It represents this so that teams can take on individual streams of related work, but at the same time, there is cohesion and consistent integration direction and workflows towards a larger, more integrated customer release.

Scrum recommends a separate backlog and a Product Owner for each team. However, how do you manage consistency, coordination, and collaboration across each of the teams? The Scrum of Scrums doesn't help in defining a *Super-set or Meta Product Backlog* [96]which is the product development strategy that will be executed across all eight of those teams.

Instead, this challenge falls squarely on the shoulders of the Product Owners, albeit at a different level; the enterprise-scale product and road-map levels. Usually, in larger scale agile instances, there is a Product Management organization that includes multiple Product Owners. More often than not, a Chief Product Owner will lead this group and be responsible for broad product feature sets, delivery road-maps, forecasting release commitments, achievement of quality targets, and overall product consistency.

It's this Chief Product Owner who creates and maintains that higher level (Meta) product backlog that drives individual team product backlogs and, subsequently, the Scrum teams. They're also responsible for scaling and growing the Product Owner organization, which leads to cross backlog and

---

[96] I like to use the term Meta Product Backlog, but it's not that common in the community. I don't think there is a term for this sort of thing. I think the community in general 'overloads' the term backlog, which can be confusing whether it's at a team or cross team level.

cross Product Owner interactions and effective collaboration within the Scrum of Scrums structure.

Many agile organizations fail to scale their agile instances at the product level as much as they do at the development team level. They simply miss the need for it, thinking that a disparate group of Product Owners should be able to "work amongst themselves" to integrate the work. While this can work in small instances, it doesn't scale well. I'd also argue that these larger scale organizations know very well how to operate with larger product planning and coordination. They just think agility relieves them of this hard work; which couldn't be more untrue.

Chief Product Owner – Office of the Product Owner

In the last chapter we explored scaling the organization and the role of Scrum of Scrums. In this chapter, we will touch on what role the *Chief Product Owner*[97] plays in effectively scaling the Product Owner organization; creating one that can support the growing instances of Scrum being used for product development.

A large part of that scaling isn't simply collaborating with the Scrum of Scrums and feeding the teams a backlog. Instead, it surrounds creating a Product Owner organization that has the depth, breadth, and skills required to support their agile teams, while _still_ supporting traditional product management responsibilities.

One mechanism to help do this would be to create an _Office of the Product Owner_ which somewhat mirrors the Product Management Office (PMO) and Scrum of Scrums, but from a pure product management perspective. This would be the function and team that would support all aspects of instantiating agility within your product teams.

This is where you'd take a hard look at individual capabilities and decide how you can, and should, support the agile team requirements; with single Product Owners, or combinations of individuals, that meet the skill-set requirements.

---

[97] Just to be clear, the Chief Product Owner is usually an adjunct title or role assigned to a senior member of the Product organization. In the story on the next page, the CPO at iContact was the Director of Product Management. Very often either Director or VP-level individuals take on these important roles.

You'd also assess skill sets and setup training and mentoring programs to ensure that your agile teams are getting the experience levels in the Product Owner role that they need to succeed. And not simply putting "names into boxes".

It's also the function where you build an effective organization of product ownership, regardless of how many individual Product Owners and/or Product Managers you need. For example, I've seen product organizations hire traditional business analysts to fill the skills-set and team needs for developing user stories and other forms of requirements. They've even brought User Experience (UX) skills to help define more useable systems.

It's the Chief Product Owners responsibility to develop their organization to effectively meet all of the external marketing demands and the internal agile demands of the organization. Let's explore some options via a few stories.

iContact, A 2+ Year Product Evolution Story

I worked at iContact from 2009 through early 2012. It was a Scrum-based organization composed of about 10-12 Scrum and Kanban teams. In parallel with the technology organization, there was a separate product organization. Product Marketing & Management was where all of the Product Owners fell and there was a Director of Product Management. For most of my time, the Product Marketing group fell under the VP of Marketing.

Over that two year span we tried three basic models for 'connecting' Product Owners to their Scrum teams. We learned a lot during the process and eventually struck upon a model that worked well for us.

Phase 1 – Every Product Manager was reframed as a Product Owner. While they still had their responsibilities towards external product marketing as a product manager, we basically overloaded them with the role of Product Owner. Over time, we noticed that they couldn't "keep up" with their overall responsibilities. And usually, their Scrum team suffered from the workload imbalance; meaning they weren't there for their teams and the teams' results would suffer.

Phase 2 – We began to separate the responsibilities of Product Managers (externally focused) and Product Owners (team focused). We started massaging job and role descriptions to ensure that the responsibilities were clear. Since we were understaffed in our product organization, we focused more on Product Owners, making a conscience decision to expose our lack of external product marketing for a short while. We also "over loaded" our Product Owners with two teams each. We found that this was an efficient model that we stayed with for the longer team. In fact, the Product Owners were central to this decision.

Phase 3 – We began recruiting more externally focused Product Managers on that side of the organization. We also created a hierarchical relationship between Product Managers and Product Owners, in that a PM would have multiple PO's loosely reporting to them along product boundaries. In this case, the PM would be the visionary, and set the overall plans and forecasts for each of their product lines. The PO's would be tactically focused towards translating high level needs to streams of user stories; then doing sprint and release planning with their respective teams.

Before phase three we had some morale challenges with the PO's in that they felt the agile Product Owner model was limiting and that there was no place for them to go within the product organization. As we evolved, more opportunities opened up for product team members to either take on more or new teams from a PO perspective or move into a PM role with it's very difference set of challenges and inherent external visibility and growth.

Ending the story, we felt that things were working well in our latest model and we stayed with it.

As an aside, I've seen this evolution towards phase three as a resilient structure quite a few times in my coaching. I think it's a pattern many organizations are discovering that works quite nicely.

While it does require an investment in people, *hiring more Product Managers and Owners*[98], it turns out to be a worthwhile investment because

---

[98] There's often a great reluctance in many organizations to hire Product Owners when adopting Scrum. The same reluctance appears when hiring Scrum Masters. Many leaders feel as if it's a 'waste' to hire these additional and new roles and would prefer to cobble together existing team members into these roles. This overloading of roles is one of the leading failure factors in Scrum adoption. Now I'm not saying you can't reframe some of your existing team member roles, but you

of how important the product organization is in guiding agile results. Now here's another story on how a company handled the same challenge.

Story – BA's as Product Owners

Another common pattern I'm seeing in several of my clients in 2011-2012 is staffing Scrum team Product Owners with traditional Business Analysts (BA). Usually the technical organization provides the BA's in the equation, so there is some consistency in staffing the Scrum teams.

The BA's then have a dotted-line reporting structure to a Product Manager (PM) in the product organization. Typically there are multiple BA's per Product Manager, say on the order of 3-5, which equates to the number of teams contributing to that product or product area.

This is somewhat aligned with the structure in phase 3 of the previous story. However, it can suffer from several challenges that need to be addressed in order for the model to be effective.

The business analysts need sufficient domain knowledge and a shared vision from the PM in order to effectively represent them. Their decisions also need to be 'sticky'. For example, they can't always have to ask permission of their PM before making everyday decisions or they'll demoralize their team with their ineffectiveness. So, the PM's in these cases need to collaborate with and effectively share their product vision and decision-making capacity with the BA's. They need to trust them as well.

The other important point is that the PM's need to remain engaged with the teams. They can't view the BA as their surrogate to the point where they become uninvolved. Instead, they need to attend many of the Scrum ceremonies and be fully vested in their teams' progress. This is particularly important when the teams are doing release-level envisioning and planning.

---

have to honor the importance of having focused Product Owners and focused Scrum Masters in your adoption.

And finally, here's a comment from Michael Faisst that is another example of the evolutionary movement going on in the Agile Product Management space.

Story – Michael's In versus Outbound Role

One point of feedback, I see an evolutionary change between the first and second editions of the book in the way product ownership is organized in companies moving towards agile methods.

Between 2003 and 2008, most organizations seemed intrigued but unsure about how useful the idea was of splitting product ownership between an inbound Product Owner (Business Analyst like) co-located with the team and an outbound Product Manager (traditional product management). The typical response always seemed to be a unified role, with the Product Owner struggling to "keep up".

Since early 2011 every software organization doing 'agile' that I've spoken too has started to parse the role into an inbound versus outbound model. They've spoken of inbound Product Management versus Outbound Product management; Product Owners versus Solution Managers or even Product Managers versus Product Directors.

They all shared how challenging it is in agile domains balancing your time between your internal teams and your market/customers. People either spend all their time on the road talking to customers, press, and analysts and as a result not being available enough to their team (missing scrums, late replies to questions from the team, etc.) or they spend too much time with the team having others in the organization become the expert on what the market wanted/needed.

Reasons were often the "Squeaky wheel syndrome" (sales, customers, development or anyone who was best at getting the PM's attention. With natural tendencies came into play as well, with Product Owners aligning with the people they felt most 'comfortable'; either the team or customers.

This new organizational alignment seems to be working well and creating high-impact, high-value products without 'killing' the Product Owners.

Distributed Teams – Requirement Artifacts

One of the common perceptions surrounding agility is that it's documentation-lite; particularly in the area of requirements. That's essentially true, but mostly driven from the needs within smaller team and project contexts. In a far more broad set of contexts, agile teams actually need to increase their requirements and other artifacts, both in size and in earlier development. This places very traditional requirement writing pressure on the Product Owner and on the team. What are some of those contexts?

1. **Larger teams and/or Distributed teams:** As teams scale, face-to-face communication and collaboration breaks down in its effectiveness and feasibility. You simply can't be as effective and there are too many communication channels.

2. **Volatile teams:** In these cases I'm speaking of attrition, either by *M&A activity*[99], growth and/or true attrition based on market conditions. The truth is, if you have high turnover in your agile teams, you need to have more artifacts to capture product and project intellectual capital for future team members to use in understanding your systems.

3. **Outsourced activities or dealing with Third Parties:** Again, you just can't expect other teams to come and interact with your teams to gain system knowledge. It's much harder to setup contracts for this approach and hold external firms accountable. Instead, define more traditional statements of work and measurable outcomes in order to allow the successful execution of external work.

4. **Regulatory or Process Requirements:** Traceability is often required in many organizations or product domains. It entails tracing requirements to code and executed test cases, verifying that you've implemented and tested what your requirement set defined. In these environments, you'll need extra rigor when defining and tracking your requirements and tests.

The above are just a few of the contexts where you need to adjust your agile artifact definition levels. There are many others. The point is that you should

---

[99] Mergers and acquisitions

be flexible in your requirement writing, but don't be fooled into thinking that meeting your context expectations as being bad or un-agile.

Instead, look to be lean in all of your artifacts. Deliver them in pieces, just-enough and just-in-time, to all of your internal partners. Importantly, instead of *pushing* work towards them, wait for them to ask for, or *pull it,* from you. That way you always deliver just what is required—and nothing more.

And There's a Co$t

Remember that as a Product Owner, you play an important part in setting the tone for requirement writing within you teams and across the broader organization. In fact, you have to be willing to "pay the cost" for your level of documentation that was committed to. For every line of documentation, you're forgoing a line of product code or a test case or a deployment utility.

Therefore, take a proactive role in understanding the 'why' behind your team documentation decisions and support the underlying value. An important part of this is placing clear and sufficient guidance in your done-ness criteria so that appropriate levels of documentation are consistently produced by your teams.

Switching gears a bit, I thought it would be useful to share a story of one Product Owner's solution to collaborating with a remote development team.

Story of a Distributed Team Interaction

In my last Scrum experience, I ran a software development team in St. Petersburg, Russia while I was in Florida. This level of distribution brought some interesting challenges to both planning and day- to-day operations. Given the time difference, I was not always readily available when the team had questions. Planning sessions had to be shortened because these intense meetings can become increasingly harder as time differences cut down on the available time window. Language differences and sound quality also made these meetings difficult to participate in.

At this point, I had decided to have a liaison on the team in the position of Product Analyst. This helped a tremendous amount as this person was available to do more leg work regarding meeting preparations and grooming the backlog, Beyond that, they helped with having a local contact that team members could talk to for clarification on specific items (since this individual had done much research on the topics that I deemed important).

However, some challenges remained. We ended up with more meetings to cover issues that had already been covered in the team's daily scrum. Mainly, because my proxy couldn't resolve the issue, or the team felt they had to explain the implications of a decision to me personally. For a while, we tried daily scrums at the end of their days yet, that seemed less productive because of the timing and requirements to discuss all topics in English, rather than just those topics that required my direct participation.

All in all, however, I wouldn't do distributed Scrum without having, at least, a liaison of the Product Owner close to the development organization.

—Michael Faisst

Distributed Teams – Tooling

There's a clear dilemma in the agile space when it comes to tooling. As the Agile Manifesto states, we'd like to emphasize *Individuals and Interactions over Process and Tools*. Many of the agile pundits, *Ron Jeffries* [100] among them, go out of their way to emphasize this point when questions regarding tools come about.

The point is that tools can often get in the way of achieving proper agile team behavior. Teams can simply follow, or trust the tools to tell them what to do, while focusing less on collaboration. I've seen this occur quite often in my coaching practice. It doesn't help that the IT world, in general, has a tendency to *throw tools* at new methods and problems, with the false hope that they'll solve everything.

At the same time, tools are a godsend when it comes to distributed team collaboration and planning within Scrum. The balance is to start early on with simple, low-fidelity cards and wall oriented planning. Perhaps, bring in some web based collaboration (Wiki's) along with Microsoft Excel. That

---

[100] I've lurked on the S*crum development* yahoo list for quite a few years and watched as Ron consistently and pointedly challenged folks on tools. His persistence in always trying to drive the thinking towards the simplest tool sets, while encouraging basic agile tenants, is not only admirable but in my view absolutely right.

way the team has some distributed support, but isn't leaning too heavily on those tools.

Once you've got some experience and maturity in agile collaboration, begin looking at some of the more powerful solutions for agile tooling. Here's a short list of tools that might prove helpful in these cases and, in no particular order, including:

- Rally
- VersionOne
- Microsoft TFS
- Jira + Greenhopper
- Pivotal Tracker

My advice here would be to not lead with tools, but to plan for a tool-set once you start instantiating Scrum across your larger and distributed teams.

I'd also advise you to have a quarterly checkpoint of sorts, call it an assessment, where you examine the behavior of your teams relative to your tools usage. This will ensure that you haven't become overly dependent on these tools and that they're simply still an adjunct for your Scrum teams.

Connections to Your Stakeholders

It's fairly easy to maintain your transparency and connectedness to your stakeholders in small instances of agility. Keeping your stakeholders effectively engaged at scale can be much tougher.

We spoke about one aspect of that engagement earlier in the book – surrounding the importance of getting key stakeholders to attend your sprint reviews. In the larger context case, that probably means you're conducting remote or distributed reviews. While it might be daunting to schedule or set these up, broad inclusion becomes even more important at scale.

Leverage distributed meeting technology to display your review for remote attendees. Make sure you give early enough notice so all can attend. Most importantly, make it clear as to what you're delivering and why, from a value perspective. Generate some excitement to get their attention and attendance.

If you know a key stakeholder is busy, reach out to them and ask for a delegate. Or, send them a *recording*[101] or minutes following the review so they can clearly understand what went on. In a larger scale, maintain effective customer connectivity

Distributed Stand-ups

To take this idea a step further, please try and make all of your Scrum meetings highly accessible. For example, setup a conference call for folks to listen in to your daily Scrum. Occasionally, use a video link for daily standups and sprint planning meetings. You'll receive a positive return for any effort you make to simulate small team agile behavior for larger, more broadly distributed teams.

Borrowing an 'Old' Idea

In traditional project planning, there's the notion of a communications plan; where a project manager will define roles and responsibilities for effectively communicating project state across the team and around to stakeholders. You do this as part of project chartering – so very early in the project.

What's useful about the technique is that you define your key communications channels (people, needs, methods) early, and establish a communications commitment on the part of your team members and key stakeholders. While it's not perfect, it may help you to connect to your stakeholders, particularly if they're accustomed to the technique. So talk to your Scrum Master as you might want to try this in your agile context.

---

[101] At iContact our executive team was often traveling. While they were VERY interested in our sprint reviews and in giving feedback, they simply had other things to attend to. We began to video tape our sprint reviews—entirely. Then they could view those areas where they had the most interest at a convenient time. We found that this improved our overall transparency and feedback. And at the same time, nobody used it as an excuse for not attending or not delegating.

Wrapping Up

❖ While I don't have a silver bullet solution, I see a very common pattern where Product Owner organizations lag all others in agile organizational adoption. Since they're so crucial, the reverse should be the standard. I can't emphasize enough the need for a Chief Product Owner and Meta-Backlogs when you start to scale.

❖ No matter how many different methodologies or Project Management Office structures you deal with, try to maintain your agile Scope trade-off dynamics and don't allow Quality to be compromised instead. You'll go slower of you do!

❖ It will be tempting to simply *throw tools* at your agile scaling challenges. While they play a part in it, don't lose your agile basics on collaboration and communication in lieu of applying a complex, distributed tool.

Chapter 20

Wrapping Up

Phew!

I think I'm done.

The first edition of the book had about 180 pages of content. The second edition has approximately 240. While that's only a 60 page difference, I feel like the second edition has taken nearly as long to develop and write as the first.

The hardest part was trying to figure out what to keep, what to remove, and what to add. All while keeping an eye towards the prime directive for the book; that of being THE reference for effective Scrum Product Ownership.

To that end, I hope you found some value in the updates and the overall book. As with any Product Owner, value to you as my 'customer' is my primary motivation.

You Rock!

Next I want to 'appreciate' you for your role. It's an incredibly tough role within Scrum teams. It's subtle, nuanced, and situational. Don't let anyone tell you that it's easy or trivialize the role.

I want to thank you for taking it on in your Scrum teams and for endeavoring to be great. Your teams may not always say it, but I'm sure they appreciate your efforts as well. Don't ever forget that they're your partners in this journey.

Feedback

My hope is that this short guide provided some valuable insights and ideas on how you might become a Great Product Owner. However, it was never intended to be exhaustive or prescriptive in nature. If you've learned one thing in your agile experience and reading, the learning primarily comes in the *doing*.

If in your *doing* you find things you want to add or change in the text, please send them to me. While I intend to keep it pragmatic, short, and approachable, I'd enjoy hearing your experiences, changes, comments, ideas, virtually anything from the agile community that might improve this guide for the next edition.

My driving intention in writing this was to help, so if I can inspect and adapt towards improvement…that's the point.

Please send all such commentary to: bob@rgalen.com. You can also connect with me via LinkedIn http://www.linkedin.com/in/bobgalen if you wish to stay in touch and network via that mechanism.

And finally, I plan on pulling together an Agile Product Owner discussion group for readers of the group. At the moment, I don't know if the group will be Google, LinkedIn, or Yahoo based. You can check here to find out more – http://www.rgalen.com/books-references/ and please join the discussions…

Cheers!
Bob.

Author Background

Robert 'Bob' Galen is an Agile Methodologist, Practitioner and Coach based in Cary, NC. In this role he helps guide companies and teams in their pragmatic adoption and organizational shift towards Scrum and other Agile methods and practices. He is currently President and Principal Consultant at RGalen Consulting Group, LLC.

Bob regularly speaks at international conferences and professional groups on topics related to software development, project management, software testing and team leadership. He is a Certified Scrum Coach (CSC), Certified Scrum Product Owner (CSPO), and an active member of the Agile Alliance & Scrum Alliance.

- In 2004 he published the book _Software Endgames – Eliminating Defects, Controlling Change and the Countdown to On-Time Delivery_ with Dorset House. The books' focus is how to successfully _finish_ your software projects.

- In 2009 he published the book _Scrum Product Ownership – Balancing Value from the Inside Out_. The book addresses the gap in guidance towards effective agile product management. This is the 2'nd edition of that book.

- In 2012 he published the book _Agile Reflections – Musings Toward Becoming "Seriously Agile" in Software Development_. The book is a compilation of blog posts from BA Times and PM Times sites from 2009 thru 2012.

Appendix A

Primer for Acceptance Test Driven Development

One of more powerful developments within the agile methods is all of the momentum driven by those lowly acceptance tests surrounding user stories. Believe it or not, an entire community of tools and thinking emerged from these simple conditions of acceptance.

I wanted to share some information surrounding this trend as it does impact Product Owners who are crafting their backlogs. In the extreme case, your teams will want you to write your acceptance tests in a specific format so that the tooling can convert and run them automatically.

Also, the writing of the acceptance tests will become almost a continuous process; not only before a story is injected into a sprint for execution, but receiving particular attention *during* story development. So, your engagement levels and time investment might increase as well.

The intent of this appendix is to serve as a simple reference or primer. Entire books have been written on the topic, so I'm not trying to replace them. In essence, I'm simply trying to make you aware of the trend and give you a baseline understanding.

WARNING: There is a technical nature to ATDD and the related tooling / approaches. Don't let that put you off. It's worth your time to immerse in the concepts with your team!

Terminology

- **Acceptance Criteria or Acceptance Test**: a series of business-centric tests associated with each User Story. If you remember the 3-C's for user stories from Chapter 9, acceptance tests are the confirmation part of the story. I typically look for 3-5 to no more than 8 crisply defined tests that are the "conditions for acceptance" on the part of the Product Owner for the story.

- **User Acceptance Tests (or UAT)**: traditional UAT has virtually nothing to do with ATDD. The two are apples and oranges; so don't muddy the two together.

- **Test-Driven Development (or TDD)**: originated from the Extreme Programming community and relates to writing and automating *unit tests* as part of the development process. The novel idea with TDD was to leverage it as a design approach by writing your unit tests *before* you wrote the code. So they would first fail (Red) and then pass as you wrote elements of the code (Green). And yes, you would have a robust level of unit tests to re-run as a result too.

- **Acceptance Test-Driven Development (or ATDD)**: This is a spinoff of the TDD idea. Now though, you would write acceptance-level (and functional level) tests as a means of exploring your requirements while developing each user story. Again, the tests would be 'driving' the functionality AND the collaboration around each story.

  Sometimes you hear the notion of "executable requirements" being referenced as ATDD. And in this case, the tests are automated with one of the rich open source tools that facilitate the activity.

- **Behavior-Driven Development (or BDD)**: This is simply a variant of ATDD that has risen mostly from the Cucumber community. It's a specific style of crafting or writing your acceptance tests. There's the notion of writing them in Gherkin format; of which there will be later examples. Gherkin has established a **Given – When – Then** format for acceptance conditional writing.

- **The Triad**: As I mentioned in Chapter 18, the Triad is a concept that is coupled with the partnership aspects naturally associated with acceptance tests. The triad is the Product Owner + Tester(s) + Developer(s) collaborating around each story from their various perspectives.

- **Specification-Driven Development**: truly comes from the Specification By Example [102] book that Gojko Adzik wrote. It puts the

---

[102] Specification by Example can be found here –
http://www.amazon.com/Specification-Example-Successful-Deliver-Software/dp/1617290084/

specification (writing) and the collaboration first; before the tooling, automation, etc. It's a reminder on how to do ATDD, BDD and this family of techniques properly.

Open Source Tooling

There are many popular open source tools in this space used to implement ATDD and BDD acceptance tests. Some of them include:

- FitNesse - ATDD
- JBehave - BDD
- RSpec - BDD
- SpecFlow - BDD
- Cucumber, Cuke4Duke, Cuke4Nuke - BDD
- Robot Framework - ATDD
- Selenium and Watir/Watin: plug-ins for Web based testing

Robot Framework: Table-Drive ATDD

Both the Robot Framework and FitNesse are examples of table driven acceptance test frameworks. These are where specific table formats are setup to drive specific row-wise tests within your application.

This is an example from Wikipedia entry for ATDD here - http://en.wikipedia.org/wiki/Robot_Framework

With the help of the SeleniumLibrary,[5] writing tests for web applications is very easy too:

Open Browser	http://www.google.com	ie[clarification needed]
Input Text	id=lst-ib	Robot Framework
Click Button	Google Search	

This test opens a new browser window and performs an internet search for the term "Robot Framework". While very simply you get a quick flavor for the table driven nature of the "test steps".

Cucumber – Gherkin: BDD Example

The Gherkin 'language' is specific to Cucumber, but since cucumber has become so popular, Gherkin has become a nearly ubiquitous way of describing BDD acceptance tests. It is characterized by its: Given-When-Then syntax for writing tests.

This is an example from the Wikipedia entry for BDD here:
http://en.wikipedia.org/wiki/Behavior-driven_development

> **User Story: Returns go to stock; In order to keep track of stock**
>
> **As a** store owner
> **I want to** add items back to stock when they're returned
> (note: there is no "So that" clause here...)
>
> **Scenario 1:** Refunded items should be returned to stock
> **Given**   a customer previously bought a black sweater from me
> **And**   I currently have three black sweaters left in stock
> **When**   he returns the sweater for a refund
> **Then**   I should have four black sweaters in stock
>
> **Scenario 2:** Replaced items should be returned to stock
> **Given**   that a customer buys a blue garment
> **And**   I have two blue garments in stock
> **And**   three black garments in stock.
> **When**   he returns the garment for a replacement in black,
> **Then**   I should have three blue garments in stock
> **And**   two black garments in stock

The HOPE

Why did I even write this appendix? It sounds like this is much more of a test automation play than a user story or software requirement play.

Well it is and it isn't.

Yes, the tools are "techy" and yes, they do potentially, support lots and lots of automation. But the hope of ATDD is increased customer collaboration with the team; leading to more collaborative and illustrative requirements. Requirements that lead to better products that delivers additional value to their customers.

That's the hope, not automation, but value-driven products. Now if we could only get those pesky Triad's to communicate...

A Final Story – Too Many Cucumbers

I was coaching a client who had been building Cucumber – BDD level acceptance tests and functional tests quite actively as part of their Scrum adoption.

They were a world-wide financial firm that had been doing Scrum for about a year. They were unique in their adoption in that they were adopting a very specific set of practices that weren't necessarily holistic. And it was causing them all sorts of *adoption health problems*[103].

For example, they went "All In" on BDD with Cucumber. They had some seasoned agile trainers come in and do developer and team training on BDD. They adopted it across a large set of their teams. Since they viewed it as an acceptance test but ALSO a functional test play, their teams literally wrote thousands of Cucumber tests.

That's good right?

Well, the down-side was that they were behind the curve on writing solid user stories. In fact, many of the teams didn't understand how to write, decompose, effectively estimate, or even how to write effective acceptance tests on their stories. So you might ask, how were they writing the BDD tests without solid user stories?

Well, because they more so considered them functional automation. And they missed the _whole point_ of BDD. It's not to write test automation. It is a means for the team to effectively collaborate around, explore, and then implement high-value solutions to their customers' challenges.

Please don't fall into this same trap. Remember: Stories – first. Collaboration – first. Triad – first. Specification-driven conversations – first. Automation – second.

---

[103] In fact, this client inspired me to write this blog post which focuses on the proper initiation of agile practices AND the "cost of entry" or applying a more meaningful set of them when you're just starting out.

More here: http://www.rgalen.com/blog/2012/5/28/the-agile-project-managergoing-agilethe-price-of-admission.html

Appendix B

The 'Smells' of Well-Groomed Backlogs

1. Sprint planning is incredibly crisp, short and easy; usually taking 2 hours or less for a 2-week sprint. There are NO architectural or design discussions within the meeting – the relevant parts of these discussions having occurred earlier.

2. As a daily occurrence, team members are talking about epics and stories targeted for 2-3-4 sprints in the future. As a result, everyone is naturally aligning with the Product Owners' vision.

3. The team easily contributes new stories to the backlog which represents non-feature based work; for example: testing artifacts, non-functional testing work, refactoring, automation development, performance tuning, research spikes, etc. Everyone views it as a shared responsibility.

4. The team has a feel for where the product is going long term and maps efforts, designs, theme suggestions, and trade-offs towards that vision.

5. Each sprint's goal is easily derived from the backlog; i.e., there is a sense of thoughtful and meaningful story collections or themes that easily surface from within the backlog. From time to time, think of these as "packages" for customer delivery.

6. The Product Owner includes team feedback (bugs, refactoring, improvement, testing, etc.) in EVERY sprint—in some percentage of focus. They clearly show the team that they are listening and acting on their feedback, judgment, and technical opinions.

7. The Product Owner rarely changes priority of elements purely because of size estimates. This doesn't include breaking them into "now versus later" bits. Illustrating that priority is mostly driven from external business needs that are translated into stories.

8. Blitz planning is done every 2-3 weeks, not only as a planning tool, but also as a risk or adjustment tool. For XP folks, consider release planning as being a similar exercise. The point is end-to-end planning towards the next release milestone occurs iteratively and frequently.

9. Teams are hitting stretch items and pulling in more work per sprint. There is an enthusiasm to deliver more towards goals by creatively trading off story sub-elements. Of course, all of this is heavily collaborated with the Product Owner.

10. The backlog is mapped to the teams' skills and capabilities, stretching them – yes, but not asking them to do things they are not capable of doing either by skill or experience.

11. Within every sprint, the Product Owner is making micro-adjustments to scope based on interactions with the team. Always striving for that Minimal Marketable Feature and Product set!

12. The team is never surprised in sprint planning. Not even by a single story. I know, change is supposed to happen, but surprising the team with last minute changes…is not! Instead, make it wait till the next sprint.

13. The team feels they have a say in what's on the backlog and the distribution of features vs. improvement items. However, they can't be solely parochial in their views. They need to make a business case from the customers' point of view, for all non-feature work introduced into the backlog; they do this willingly and effectively!

Appendix C

Product Owner: Desk References

A very short list of practical books that provide guidance that is relevant for the Great Product Owner. Every one of these should be on your bookshelf!

1. Lyssa Adkins, *Coaching Agile Teams: A Companion for Scrum Masters, Agile Coaches, and Project Managers in Transition*
2. **Marty Cagan, *Inspired: How to Create Products Customers Love*
3. **Greg Cohen, *Agile Excellence for Product Managers: A Guide to Creating Winning Products with Agile Development Teams*
4. **Mile Cohn, *User Stories Applied – For Agile Software Development*
5. Mike Cohn, *Agile Estimating and Planning*
6. Mike Cohn, *Succeeding with Agile: Software Development Using Scrum*
7. Esther Derby and Diana Larsen, *Agile Retrospectives: Making Good Teams Great*
8. **Henrik Kniberg, *Scrum and XP From the Trenches*
9. Henrik Kniberg, *Kanban and Scrum – Making the Most of Both*
10. Henrik Kniberg, *Lean from the Trenches: Managing Large-Scale Projects with Kanban*
11. **Diana Larsen and Ainsley Nies, *Liftoff: Launching Agile Teams & Projects*
12. Dean Leffingwell, *Scaling Software Agility – Best Practices for Large Enterprises*
13. Dean Leffingwell, *Agile Software Requirements: Lean Requirements, Practices for Teams, Programs, and the Enterprise*
14. **Eric Ries, *The Lean Startup: How Todays Entrepreneurs Use Continuous Innovation to Create Radically Successful Businesses*
15. **Kenny Rubin, *Essential Scrum: A Practical Guide to the Most Popular Agile Process*
16. Gojko Adzic, *Test Driven .Net Development with FitNesse*
17. **Gojko, Adzic, *Bridging the Communication Gap: Specification by Example and Agile Acceptance*
18. **Gojko Adzic, *Specification by Example: How Successful Teams Deliver the Right Software*
19. David Celimsky, Dave Astels, Bryan Helmkamp, and Dan North, *The RSpec Book: Behavior Driven Development with RSpec, Cucumber, and Friends*
20. Markus Garnter, *ATDD by Example: A Practical Guide to Acceptance Test-Driven Development*
21. **Ken Pugh, *Lean-Agile Acceptance Test-Driven Development: Better Software Through Collaboration*
22. Matt Wynne and Aslak Hellesoy, *The Cucumber Book: Behavior-Driven Development for Testers and Developers*

** - an even smaller subset; and of course, this book as well.

Appendix D

Assessing the Product Organization and the Product Owner

Bill Krebs [104]has introduced an agile maturity measurement tool called the *Agile Journey Index or AJI*[105]. The index is intended to be used as a maturity assessment framework to guide the evolution, the journey if you will, of agile teams.

It has a skew towards Scrum terminology and practices, but literally crosses all three of the major agile methods: Scrum, XP, and Kanban in their normal implementations. Bill worked at IBM for years, helping them to roll-out agility, so the seeds of the AJI were developed during quite a large-scale adoption effort.

Bill is now working at AllScripts as an agile coach and has refined the AJI to the point where's he's currently writing a book on the topic. It should be available mid-year 2013.

Now let me clear. I don't think grading systems should be applied to agile teams. Nor should teams be contrasted one against the other. Teams are unique and grades are simply not helpful; particularly in larger scale organizations.

But you have to ask the questions:
- How are we doing?
- What are our strengths? And our weaknesses?
- And most importantly, where should we be focusing our improvement?

---

[104] In the agile community he is better known as AgileBill Krebs – www.linkedin.com/in/billkrebs

[105] More information here: http://www.agiledimensions.com/blog/2011/10/agile-journey-index/

And having a tool that helps define a landscape of questions and levels of maturity can be incredibly helpful in guiding a teams or an organizations evolution - their journey.

Extension to the AJI for Product Ownership

To that end, I've extended the AJI for evaluating the Agile Product Organization and individual Product Owners. I've done that primarily to provide a set of maturity guidelines to help you in guiding your Agile Product Team evolution. I also use it in my coaching to provide product-level organizational assessments.

If you want to get a copy of the Product Owner AJI-extensions, simply email me with that request. By doing so, you promise to use the information wisely and in the true spirit of agile continuous improvement.

I'll also ask you to provide me with anonymous AJI information afterwards so that I can begin to create a "maturity index" of the agile product community. I think this will help everyone in understanding where particular challenges reside and how we're maturing as a 'practice'.

As a friend always tells me after attending the annual agile conference:

I thought our organization was the only one with deep challenges and who seemed to be struggling. But we're not. There are many organizations that are much worse off than we are. Now I feel better. We're not in it alone, we've made significant progress, and we still have a ways to go.

That is the point of the Agile Journey Index, to help guide us in our Product Ownership journey. Please consider leveraging the tool and participating in the data collection and learning efforts.

Email: bob@rgalen.com and mention "AJI-Extensions" in the subject header.

Index

Made in the USA
Lexington, KY
30 January 2014